Escape Impossible

Stanley Saddington

Escape Impossible
by
Stanley Saddington

Copyright ©1997 Stanley Saddington

Published by A Lane Publishers, 61 Charles Street, Stockport SK1 3JR England

Printed and bound by Hindson Print, Newcastle-upon-Tyne, NE99 1PP

ISBN 1897666 91 3
Price £12.00 plus p/p

978189 7666913

The Author at Nefyn, North Wales 1940

Contents

Illustrations

Preface

The Burma Railway was built largely by prisoners whom the Japanese captured in Singapore, Java and Sumatra in the early months of 1942. The railway connected Thanbyuzayat in Burma with Nong Pladuk in Thailand and was about 250 miles in length. Construction was from both ends simultaneously and the junction point was Konkuita in Thailand, some 160 miles from Nong Pladuk.

Upwards of 60,000 British, Australian, Dutch and American prisoners were involved in the construction and almost half of these were British, that is to say: from the United Kingdom. Only 500 of this sizeable British contingent, however, were employed at the Burma end of the project and they consequently became known as the British Battalion. This was to distinguish them from the much larger numbers of Dutch and Australian prisoners whose various camps along the Railway, the British shared.

I was one of the British Battalion and this is mainly the story of my personal experiences with that force, though it includes also an account of the Singapore debacle, an eleventh hour attempt to evacuate some of us by sea, the sinking of the ship and our eventual capture in Sumatra.

During my captivity I travelled about two thousand miles through three countries and lived in twenty-five different prison camps. My life as a prisoner was not however, a continual round of merciless beatings. I witnessed, and indeed suffered, some violence but in my experience the main type of ill-treatment inflicted by the Japanese was deprivative. They denied us food, clothes, medicines and contact with the International Red Cross. They also, at times, grossly overworked us, particularly on the Burma Railway, where many died as a result.

The Japanese, on the whole, I found tough, aggressive and disturbingly primitive, but there were occasional instances of kindness and these I have duly recorded. I also recount some humorous incidents, though the Japanese were not often involved in these. In short, I have tried to present a balanced account of my experience which I hope may be regarded as a useful contribution to the history of the War in the Far East.

Acknowledgement

The number of British Battalion members who died both in the individual camps and in total, are derived from the late Major D P Apthorp's "British Battalion Diary", copies of which, in 1947, he was kind enough to supply both to the survivors of the Battalion and to the next of kin of those who died. The diary has since been incorporated in a book entitled "The British Sumatra Battalion", recently written by the late Major's widow, Mrs Ann Apthorp. The book includes a full nominal role of all the members of the Battalion, including rank and unit, and states the date and place of each of the deaths. It is therefore recommended as a more detailed source of such information and, indeed, as an alternative account of the affairs of the British Battalion.

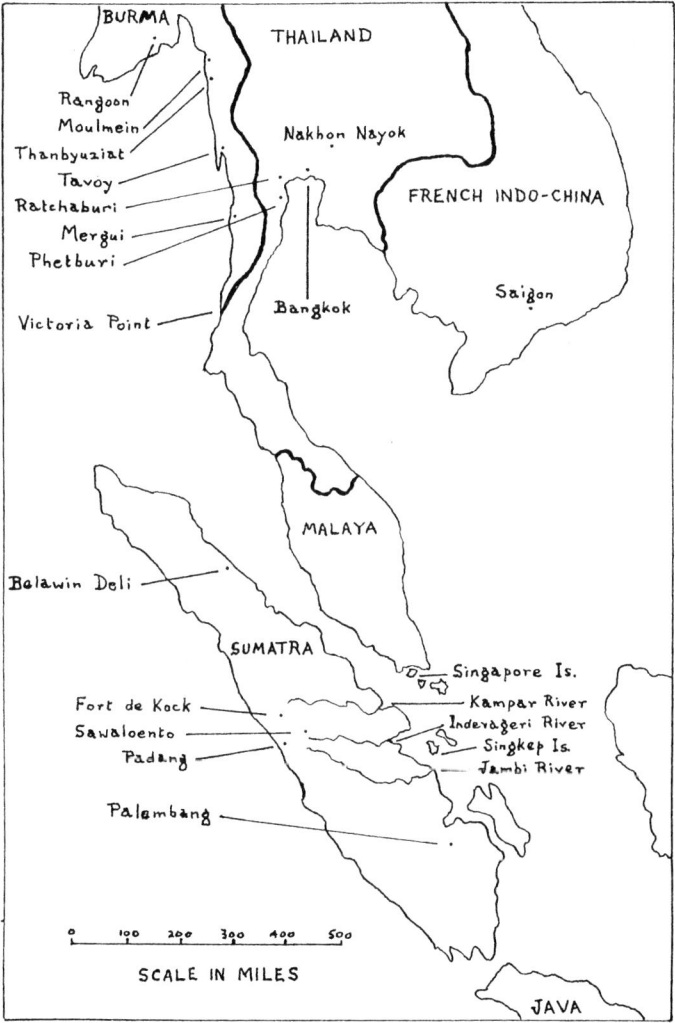

Figure 1 - Map of Malaya and Surrounding Countries

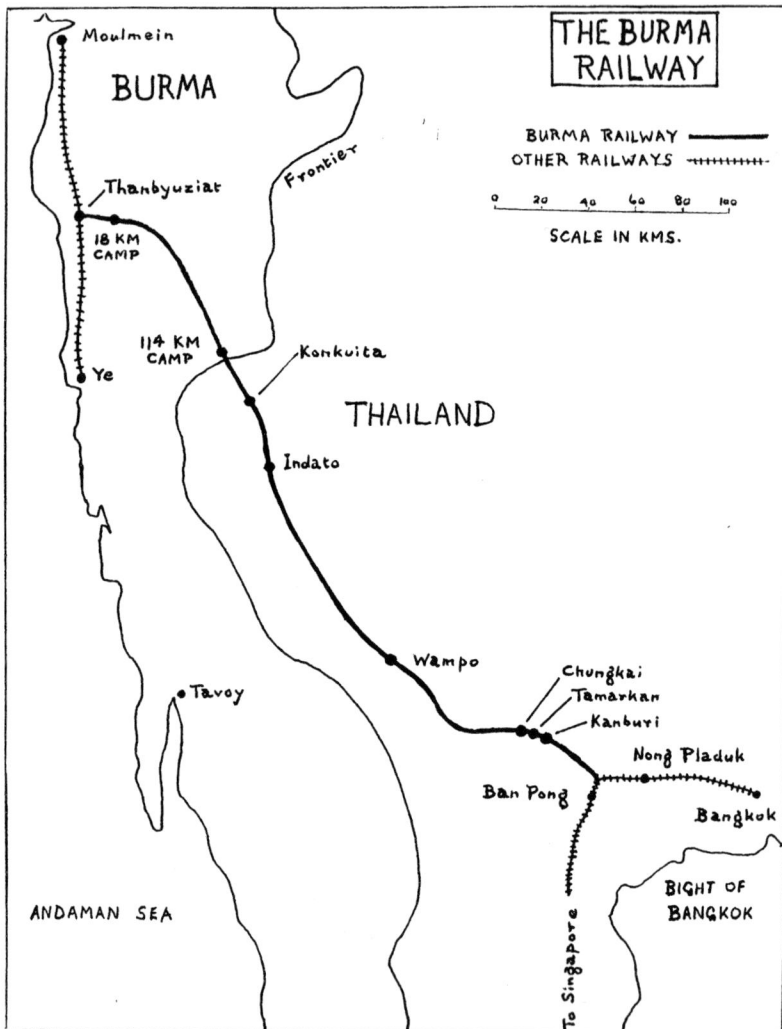

Figure 2 - The Burma Railway

Chapter One - Goodbye Singapore

It was late afternoon when the signal came through from Air Headquarters. We were to destroy and evacuate our radar station within half an hour. The order was neither surprising nor unwelcome. From the outset, the war in Malaya had been one losing battle after another, and now the Japanese had not only taken the whole of the mainland but also gained a powerful lodgement on Singapore Island. Since this landing on the north-west shore of the island. four days previously, information had been scant and unreliable and none of us at the radar station knew exactly where the front line was. We knew that the ultimate objective of the Japanese was the port and city of Singapore, which lies on the southern side of the island, but how near they now were to their goal we could not tell. Nor did we know whether the enemy was driving straight for Singapore, or was fanning eastward across the island before making his final assault on the city. Our station was in the north-east of the island, isolated, small and ill-defended. Our total complement was about a dozen, half of us either radar mechanics or operators, the rest guards of various trades. We each had a rifle and fifty rounds and the guards, in addition, had two Thompson sub-machine guns. Thus equipped, and having no combat experience or training, we would have been easy meat for even a platoon of battle hardened Japanese infantry, and none of us was therefore anxious for engagement. It also occurred to me that, if we should fall into enemy hands alive, there would be some awkward questions regarding the nature of our job and, under the kind of persuasion which the Japanese were said to employ, it would be difficult not to disclose some very valuable information. Small wonder then that, when the order came to bail out, we were not slow to comply.

The transmitter and receiver were quickly switched off. We then attacked them with hammers. We smashed every valve and every component, with particular attention to the cathode ray tubes which, if discovered intact, would have proclaimed the nature of the station more clearly than anything. Their glass parts we battered into unrecognisable fragments and their metal bases we mutilated and buried. Next we dealt with the diesel generator. While it was still running, we poured sand into its fuel tank and, when it finally laboured to a halt, we fell upon it with hammers, battering, breaking and bending as many of its working parts as we could uncover. The final job was to set fire to the wooden huts. There were three of them. One was a barrack, one housed the transmitter, and the third the receiver. We soaked them with petrol and flung a bundle of burning rags into each doorway. In seconds the buildings were roaring, crackling bonfires. We jumped onto the lorry and rapidly departed to the accompaniment of exploding .303 ammunition which the guards had inadvertently left behind in the barrack hut.

As we jolted along the track that led out of the rubber plantation, I fell to wondering whether our activities at the radar station had been of any real value. The equipment had been installed in a great hurry and certainly not functioned as effectively as it should have done. Our aerials in particular were inadequate. Instead of being mounted, as was normal, on hundred foot towers, they had been supported on thirty foot telegraph poles and had barely peeped above the tops of the rubber trees. I do not know whether the height of the aerials had purposely been restricted in order to escape observation from the air and from the enemy occupied mainland across the straits, or whether the customary masts had simply not been available, but whatever the reason the result had been a drastic reduction in our performance. The most obvious effect was a reduction of our range from a hundred miles or more, to barely thirty. Our bearing readings had also been in considerable doubt owing to the close proximity of the tree tops and, until two days before our departure from the station, we had not been able properly to tune our aerial reflectors. This had meant we could not tell whether an aircraft flying on, for example, a north/south path, was approaching us from the north or from the south.

I also wondered what use could have been made of the intelligence(such as it was) which we had been passing to the filter room. Our chief function was to enable our fighter planes to be deployed in an effective manner, but the fighters had long since been withdrawn to Sumatra and Java - a fact made all too clear to us by an instruction from Air Headquarters stating "Regard all aircraft as enemy". This message incidentally, did nothing to bolster our morale. Our information might have been of some use to the anti-aircraft gun batteries and possibly those responsible for sounding air raid warnings in the city, but even this seemed to me doubtful. Incursions of enemy aircraft had become so frequent that I am sure both gunners and civilians must have been on constant alert.

But the job at the radar station was now over. The equipment was destroyed and we were joining the final headlong flight to the sea. There was no doubt in my mind that I was involved in the closing stages of a massive British defeat. Why, I asked myself, had we failed so miserably? Why had we retreated four hundred miles in ten short weeks? There seemed no excuse, except perhaps that our air power had been insufficient. Lack of aircraft had certainly been a factor, but whether or not it had been the critical factor I was far from certain. And how would the battle finish? Street fighting in Singapore, I presumed. Every man with a rifle in his hand. House to house skirmishing. A bloody last ditch fight to the finish, the Japanese all about us and the ocean forcing us at last to make a stand. It was a grim prospect to have to face and I found myself wondering whether an evacuation might be attempted. It had happened at Dunkirk, against equally formidable odds. Tens of thousands of troops had been snatched from the beaches of northern France. Surely a similar operation could be mounted at Singapore. But could it? We had neither airforce nor navy. There were no little ships eager to come to our aid. There was no England on our horizon. Regretfully I had to admit to myself that I was clutching at a straw. There could be no retreat from Singapore. The end would be as I had originally imagined it, a hopeless cut-throat struggle. Bayonets in the streets, sniping from the rooftops, hand grenades thrown from the darkness of alleyways and machine guns constantly dealing staccato death. It was a frightening scenario, awful to contemplate, but I could not help dwelling on it. I wondered whether my comrades had similar thoughts, but I felt it would have been out of order to enquire.

Our journey in the lorry took a long time. Apart from the blackout, which necessitated slow and careful driving, we also had to make several prolonged halts - sometimes for our identity to be checked, sometimes to join up with further RAF lorries carrying personnel from other stations. But eventually, late at night, the convoy reached its destination. No-one told us where we were but the general opinion was that we were at Kallang aerodrome, which lies on the eastern edge of Singapore city. The lorries came to rest under a tall atap roofed structure and we dismounted. The order was given to bed down and we began to make ourselves as comfortable as the cobble-stoned ground would allow. I had a groundsheet beneath me, a blanket round me and my kitbag for a pillow. The night was silent except for the rumble of distant gunfire and sleep came quickly, despite the cobblestones.

I woke at dawn. The air was chilly and I turned over in hope of a further snooze, but the lumpy ground had stiffened my limbs and I decided to get up. I hauled myself to a sitting position and looked around. We were in a draughty barn-like structure without walls, just an atap roof on tall bamboo poles. Outside, not far away, was a battered ring of sandbags which had apparently been an anti-aircraft gun emplacement. Scattered about the area were various sized wooden huts. One of them, a large one, had been half demolished by a bomb or shell and, inside I could see a wreckage of chairs and tables. I stood up, stretched, and looked further afield. To the west lay Singapore city, silent and forlorn, with remnants of smoke rising up from its bomb damaged heart. Then, high above Fort Canning, I saw the Union Jack, and patriotism took hold of me. I was proud the flag had flown here since 1819. I was proud of Raffles and I was proud of the British enterprise which had transformed the malarial swamps of Singa Pura into a prosperous city with a world-famous port. Then patriotism gave way to anger, anger that the Japanese, posing as liberators, were about to supplant us, anger that we had not made greater effort to defend the place and anger above all, at having to accept that we were vincible. Depressed by such thoughts, I hadn't much appetite. When the call to breakfast came, I was therefore inclined to ignore it but, seeing everyone else make his way towards the kitchen, I changed my mind and delved in my kitbag for cutlery and mug.

The kitchen was some distance from the camp and to reach it we had to pass through the streets of the town. As we walked along, in twos and threes, I suddenly became ware of the approaching drone of aircraft. I stopped and listened for an instant and then looked about me at my comrades. They too had heard the sound and were peering anxiously skyward. The drone of the engines grew rapidly louder.

"They're headed this way," somebody shouted.

"And there's a hell of a lot of 'em," shouted somebody else. All eyes were directed towards the throbbing hum. A moment's pause. Then, simultaneously, we saw them, about twenty bombers rapidly approaching from the east, in line abreast and flying low. Their flight path was directly over us and we scattered instinctively in search of shelter. Some lay against walls, some went in doorways, others up alleys. I chose a concrete monsoon drain. Now the bombers were overhead, filling the sky with their thunderous roar. I listened tensely for the searing rush of the bombs, heart pounding and knees like jelly. But no bombs came. The aircraft flew on and, a few seconds later, deposited their lethal cargo with a dreadful rumble on the centre of the city. We emerged from our various hidey-holes and continued on our way, conversation much subdued.

It was a good breakfast - porridge, bacon and tomatoes, and tea - but I hadn't the slightest inclination to eat. I was filled with a sense of approaching calamity and I felt dreadfully powerless. It was like trying to avoid falling over a cliff in a dream. The danger was clear, but no effort on my part was going to prevent my falling over the edge. I collected a plate of bacon and a mug of tea. The bacon nauseated me and I pushed it aside. I lit a cigarette and sipped the hot sweet tea. The combination of nicotine and caffeine was a comfort.

I walked back from the kitchen with McBain, a friend of mine. We neither of us had much to say and I formed the impression that he was as despondent as I was. On reaching the billet, we looked again at Singapore. The flag still flew but it was only fitfully visible in the smoke from the recent air raid. High in the sky above the city a single bomber circled, anti-aircraft shells exploding around it. I desperately wanted to see the bomber shot down but it continued to circle, in and out of the smoke, impervious to the gun fire. Then suddenly its nose dipped and, with engines screaming, it dived almost vertically on the city, released a single bomb, which exploded with a dull crump, and flew off, apparently unharmed.

"Good God," I said to Mac, "we can't even score one point!" Mac did his best to produce a chuckle but he was clearly not in the mood for jokes.

"Come on," he said, "let's find a place to wash."

"Right," I said, and off we went, armed with towels, etc.

The first hut we entered had apparently been an officer's bedroom, the first object to catch our eye being a well sprung mattress.

"Pity we didn't see this last night," I said to Mac.

"Yes," replied Mac, flinging himself onto the mattress and bouncing appreciatively, "I could have used this all right."

We looked round at the rest of the furnishings. There were two chairs and a chest of drawers. Some of the drawers of the chest were open. Scraps of paper and abandoned clothing were scattered about the room; a worn khaki drill shirt, an RAF belt, the remnants of a towel and a vintage sock. It looked as if the occupant had left in a hurry. In one of the drawers of the chest there was a cake - a large and rich looking fruit cake - no doubt the gift of some fond wife or mother. In another drawer lay a writing pad on the top sheet of which was a half finished letter. It assured the intended recipient that there was no cause for despondency and that "the yellow barbarian" would be speedily confounded. Mac and I admired the writer's optimism but could not bring ourselves to share it.

We left the bedroom and resumed our search for the washroom. It didn't take us long to find it. Voices and the sound of splashing water quickly led us to the room labelled "Ablutions". We looked in and were delighted at the prospect that greeted us. Washbasins, lavatories and showers. A large number of airmen were already in occupation but there was plenty of room and Mac and I went eagerly in. He started with a shower, I with a shave. The water was cold but at the age of twenty-one, and with a beard still far from mature, I did not find this any great disadvantage. Shaving finished, I washed the residue of the soap from my face and started to undress for a shower. I got as far as taking off one shoe when in came a sergeant who shouted

"Everybody on parade at the double. We're moving."

"Where to, sarge?" asked someone.

"You'll find out." replied the sergeant. "Fall in now, quick sharp."

It took some minutes for all of us to get onto the square in front of the billet, Mac particularly who had been under the shower. An officer addressed us.

"We're being evacuated," he said. "We travel down to the docks by lorry. Twenty men per vehicle. Five minute intervals. Pack your kits and fall in again here. Fall out."

The news that we were to be evacuated was music to our ears. No backs-to-the-wall street fighting after all. We packed with alacrity and were back to the square in double quick time. I had a rifle, kitbag and full webbing equipment, including two back packs, a side pack and water bottle. The officer divided us into parties of twenty and we waited for the lorries. The sun was well up and the square was hot. I expected a long wait and was in the act of composing a suitable grumble when the vehicles unexpectedly arrived. The first batch of twenty men scrambled aboard. The officer counted them as they did so, gave a signal to the driver and the lorry departed in a swirl of dust. Mine was the third vehicle.

Our journey into the city took, I suppose, about half an hour. On the way we passed a great deal of bomb damage, some of it burning. Once or twice we had to detour to avoid streets that were blocked by debris but otherwise the trip was uneventful - until we reached the dock gates. Here, as we jumped down from the lorries, we were greeted by the painful wail of air raid sirens and the sound of aircraft.

"Take cover!" shouted somebody, in a stentorian voice. We didn't need a second bidding. A drove of bombers was already thundering almost overhead and a nearby battery of anti-aircraft guns was in fierce action. Fortunately, several air raid trenches had been dug nearby and we stumbled into them just as the first of the bombs seared down. The noise they made as they tore through the air was like a hundred hellish locomotives letting off steam full blast together. Louder and louder grew the torrential hiss until I became quite certain that every single bomb was aimed at me personally. Then came the explosions, vicious staccato, earth sundering crashes that set the trench walls quivering and sent a sickening vibration through the whole of my frame. Then, abruptly, the uproar ceased. No sound but the diminishing drone of aircraft engines. The air was full of acrid fumes. Some seconds passed before the men began to emerge from the trenches. I put my hands on the parapet intending to spring nonchalantly up to ground level but alas my arms and legs were jellified and I found myself scrambling my way up without the slightest show of dignity. But I was exhilarated - exhilarated at finding myself alive and unscathed. I shall never forget that feeling of blessed relief at finding myself whole. In that moment the cares of the future disappeared like magic. I was happy simply to have survived. The rest of the party were also uninjured. All were dusty and shaken, but all were safe. We collected our baggage, fell in in twos and marched up to the dock gates.

Outside the dock gates were hundreds of civilians - Chinese, Malays, Indians and Euroasians; men, women and children - all clamouring for entrance. The sight of them filled me with pity. Many of them could have left Singapore weeks before, but they had stayed on in the faith that their homeland would never fall to the invader. Alas, the enemy was now on their doorstep. Their faith was shattered and they were in the grip of panic - panic made worse by the sight of troops being evacuated. Their cries to be let into the docks were loud and frantic. They were desperate to escape, but no-one without a permit was allowed to enter the gates. I was appalled at their plight, and ashamed that we had failed them, but I was also afraid that they would run amok. We elbowed our way slowly through them and onto the quayside.

The scene that greeted our gaze as the waterfront came into view was strange and unfamiliar. No liners towering at their berths, no goods or baggage on the quay and everywhere an unnatural quiet. I saw only three vessels which could fairly be classified as ships, and the biggest of them was a dwarf compared with the size of vessel I was used to seeing in this harbour. All three were anchored well out from the quay, and widely separated. Two appeared to be merchantmen; the other - the smallest and nearest - was flying the white ensign and was probably a gun boat or patrol ship. Thinly scattered over the rest of the harbour were a number of lesser boats, some in motion, some at anchor: a launch or two, a water-tender plying shoreward and various other minor craft. As I surveyed the scene my mind went back to the day when I had disembarked here from the 27,000 ton troopship, Capetown Castle. I saw again a host of fine ships lining the quayside and filling the harbour. I heard the rattle of busy winches, the tumble of baggage on the quay and, surmounting all other sound, the strains of "Home, Sweet Home" with which a perverted army band had greeted our arrival. What change, what contrast, five short months had wrought. Gone the great port's noisy bustle. In its stead a sinister silence broken only by the distant thud of gunfire. The prospect reeked of doom and again I had the feeling of being drawn powerless into a vortex of catastrophe.

The water tender drew alongside the quay and we were ordered to file aboard. When as many of us as possible had been crammed in, the line of waiting troops was halted and the heavily laden little vessel cast off. After a minute or two it was clear that we were heading for one of the merchantmen which I had seen from the quay. I hoped there wouldn't be another air raid while we were en route to her. Then it occurred to me that in the event of a raid, it might well be safer on the open water than on the docks. I pondered this until we reached the ship's side. She was a tiny vessel, just a few hundred tons, with one squat funnel, and she was in some need of a coat of paint. A sloping gangway had been lowered against her side and the water tender tied up at the foot of it. As we went up the gangway I noticed several ragged gashes in the hull of the ship, apparently damage from bombs or shells. She was manned by Royal Naval personnel and she had a gun, perhaps four inch, mounted in her bow. These features seemed to indicate that she was some sort of

RN auxiliary vessel, rather than a merchantman as I had first thought. Her name was Tien Kwang.

On boarding the ship, we were first taken down to the damp and dimly lit hold to stow our kitbags. When we emerged we were issued with life jackets - the chunky cork variety - and then left to our own devices. I sat down with a group of friends in a shady corner of the deck and looked across the water at the quayside we had lately left. The wharves and godowns, at that distance, looked almost intact, though rising from behind them was a thick column of smoke which the breeze was gradually spreading black and pall-like across the scene. A single aircraft, unperturbed by anti-aircraft shells which were bursting all around it, circled high above the city. I watched and waited for it to select a target and make an attack, but in a minute it straightened in its flight and made off to the north. The water tender came again, heavily loaded with more airmen. I went to the rail; watched her make fast, disgorge, cast off and head back for the quay. As she bobbed her way ponderously across the harbour I felt irritated at her slowness and wondered tetchily how many more trips she would have to make before we got underway. I watched her for what seemed an age, but she eventually merged with the land and I turned from the rail to rejoin my companions. They were sitting on the deck eating their midday meal and I decided to follow suit, but more as a diversion from the anxiety of waiting than out of any pressing desire for food. I took from my sidepack a tin of maconochie and set about opening it with my jackknife. I gingerly prised open the jaggedly cut top of the tin and began reluctantly spooning up the clammy m and v. It was revolting and I threw more than half of it overboard.

Next to me on the deck, sat Reg Bussey, a fellow radar mechanic who hailed from Islington. Reg was very tall and very thin and, as a result of these features, had been nicknamed "Pythe" - a shortened form of the word "python". Although Reg was a cockney, and had the accent to prove it, he wasn't typical. His manner was quiet and he was softly spoken. He often swore, as we all did, but his controlled delivery destroyed all offensiveness.

"Well, Stan," he said, "where to from 'ere?"

"South, I suppose," I replied. "Probably Java."

"Let's 'ope the Japs ain't there to meet us," said Reg, after a pensive pause.

"That's right," chipped in Blondie Blakelock, "be bloody cheerful."

"Not that I don't think it couldn't bloody 'appen, mind you," he added. "But it don't bear thinking about."

Blondie, also a Londoner, was rather more voluble than Reg.

Scotty, a dour young Yorkshireman took the blackest view.

"This boat's so leaky," he said, "I don't think she'll make Java anyway."

"I 'ope to God we don't sink," said Taff Jones, an eighteen year old from Lake Vyrnwy. "I can't swim."

"Swimming's not going to help anybody," said Blondie. "What good's swimming when you're miles from bloody anywhere?"

He had a point. The ability to swim in miles of ocean wasn't likely to be of great benefit. I hoped we wouldn't sink. Indeed I didn't think the ship was in such bad shape that she would sink, but the possibility was no comfort.

Figure 3 - Singapore Harbour
(largely empty)on the morning of Friday 13th February 1942.

18

Figure 4 - Singapore Harbour during the bombing attacks on Friday 13th February 1942. Taken from the deck of the auxiliary naval vessel Tien Kuang

19

Figure 5 - Singapore Harbour during the bombing attacks on Friday 13th February 1942. Taken from the deck of the auxiliary naval vessel Tien Kuang

During the long afternoon the water tender continuously plied back and forth between the dockside and the ship, bringing more and more evacuees. There were soldiers as well as airmen, and some civilians of various nationalities. Surely we would move soon. I got up and walked again to the ship's rail. I was looking particularly at a huge column of black smoke rising up from behind the docks when I suddenly became aware of the faint but unmistakable sound of approaching aircraft. There was an abrupt pause in the conversation as others around me detected the sinister sound. Then the silence was broken by the wail of air raid sirens on the shore.

"Take cover," yelled an authoritative voice, as the anti-aircraft guns began to thud. There was a pounding of feet on the steel decking as people scrambled for what shelter they could find. I tried to think where best to go, but my mind was blocked. The bombers were visible now, approaching from the north, perhaps twenty of them, in tight formation, purposeful and menacing. I lay down flat on my stomach close to a deck housing and gripped my hands tight across the back of my head. There was an agony of waiting as the rhythmic throb of the bomber engines grew ever closer. Oh for a hole in the ground! I could at least have made an attempt to get below. It was elementary that when a ship was bombed you got below, but here I was lying hopelessly exposed on the top deck. I considered making a dash for it, but the bombers were now too close. The sickening vibration of their engines filled the sky and made me grip my hands even more tightly across the back of my head. I remember also drumming my toes on the deck, so painful was the suspense. Then down rained the bombs. This was the climax, the instant when one's heart thumped fit to burst the chest, the fateful moment when one either lived or died. I lived, and so did we all on board the Tien Kwang, for the bombs had fallen mainly on the quay and godowns. Again the joy of survival. I felt as if I had recovered from a serious illness - weak but elated.

I rose from my prone position on the deck and looked across the water at the dockside. Fires were raging and heavy clouds of dark smoke were billowing upwards. As the smoke rose it covered the sun and spread a baleful twilight over the whole harbour. For some minutes I heard no sound except the distant crackle of the flames. It was as if the whole city was dead. Then, faintly, I heard the chug of a motor boat engine. It was the water tender bringing another load of evacuees. I watched her as she approached across the dark water. She carried both troops and civilians, including some children. One or two of the passengers were injured, presumably from the bombing. They came aboard grim-faced and apprehensive. A child wept miserably and would not be comforted. The tin hat of an airman had a jagged hole in its brim but the man himself was unscathed. I pondered his chances of safely reaching home to display this memento of what must have been a very lucky escape.

Refugees continued to come aboard throughout the rest of the afternoon until every nook and cranny of the little ship was occupied. Then OC Troops, a stout middle-aged group captain with a revolver in his belt, addressed us. He told us that the Tien Kwang was a flat bottomed river boat, and that any substantial movement of passengers was likely to capsize her. We were all therefore to remain in our places and anyone failing to do so would risk being shot. This somewhat dramatic warning brought forth from a lad at my elbow the muttered comment "Get fucked".

The group captain also called for two volunteer signalmen.

"What would we have to do?" asked Tommy Bouette, a friend of mine and fellow radar mechanic.

"Send Morse with an Aldis lamp," replied the group captain.

"What about it? Shall we volunteer?" asked Tom, turning to me. Tom had put the question to me because he knew that, like him, I was a keen amateur radio enthusiast and knew Morse. It hadn't occurred to me to volunteer, but I thought I might just as well do a spot of signalling as spend my time doing nothing. So I agreed and we gave our names to the group captain. He took us to a cabin where the ship's signal officer briefed us. Our job was to stand, one on the port side and one on the starboard side, of a platform in front of the bridge, watch for coded light signals from allied ships and give the appropriate code answer with our Aldis lamp. As we were taken up to the bridge and shown the platform on which we were to keep lookout, I recalled that when I had tried to

22

join the Royal Navy as a telegraphist in December 1939, I had been rejected because of short sight. This was clearly not now regarded as a serious deficiency.

We sailed at night fall in company with another small vessel called the Kuala. She also carried evacuees including a number of nurses from the Singapore hospitals. We followed the Kuala, guided by a dim blue light on her stern. My last sight of Singapore was three large fires glowing in the darkness towards the western edge of the island. It was Friday, the thirteenth of February, 1942.

Chapter Two - Attacked at Sea

The night was silent except for the steady churning of our engines and the faint swishing of our bow wave. It was cold standing on the open platform in front of the bridge, Tom on the starboard side, I on the port. We had blankets round our shoulders but we were high above the waterline and there was a continuous wind which chilled us to the marrow. Hours went by and we saw nothing except the pale blue stern light of the Kuala, and even that at times disappeared.

I was disappointed that no allied shipping crossed our path. The appearance of a Royal Navy vessel would have greatly reassured me. I was glad, however, that the sea appeared equally empty of enemy ships. The thought of meeting a Japanese warship appalled me. I imagined the situation. She would challenge us. We would not know the code letters with which to reply. There would be a short and awful pause. Then, inevitably, a broadside which would send us to the bottom.

I was torturing myself with these thoughts when the Signals Officer appeared and told us to send a signal to Kuala requesting a brighter stern light. I realised that we had had difficulty in following the Kuala, but I was surprised by the order to signal her and thus risk attracting enemy attention. However, in the armed forces one didn't question orders, and the signal was duly sent. The Kuala acknowledged and brightened her stern light, but not much, which I thought was very wise.

The Signals Officer departed and Tom and I resumed our watch. But a few minutes later the Signals Officer returned and told us once again to signal the Kuala, this time to advise her that one of our engines had broken down and that our maximum speed was thus reduced to five knots. Kuala was required to slow down accordingly. I sent the signal and, after what seemed a very long pause, Kuala acknowledged and agreed to comply. The Signals Officer then left us again, saying as he went that cocoa would be "coming in a minute". It duly arrived in two large white mugs brought by a seaman. It was hot and sweet and very comforting, but I kept thinking about the breakdown of the engine. How reliable was the other one(I presumed we had two) and what would happen to us if it also gave up the ghost? Such thoughts, in the darkness and cold, depressed me and made it increasingly difficult to keep effective watch. I found myself too often staring in one direction instead of methodically scanning the blackness.

The darkness and cold seemed interminable. The normal length of a watch is four hours but since, apparently, Tom and I were the only signalmen available there was no hope of any relief and we were therefore at our post throughout the night. When at last the sun rose and once again began to glint upon the water the two ships dropped anchor in the bay of a small island. This was Pom Pong, one of the hundreds of Dutch islands which dot the sea to the south of Singapore. It seemed about a mile in length, was steep sided and heavily covered in trees. How far it lies from Singapore I still do not know, for I have never seen a map of large enough scale to include such a tiny dot of land, but I estimate that during the night we covered perhaps seventy miles. In the distance other islands were visible and, almost on the horizon, there was a third ship, motionless and apparently abandoned.

The plan was to remain at anchor during the daylight, in order to escape observation, and to sail under cover of darkness. Judging from our experience so far, night travel seemed safe enough, but I was not so convinced that it was wise to remain motionless in daylight. If spotted, the two ships would be sitting ducks. The crew of a native fishing boat which had been at anchor on our arrival at Pom Pong had clearly thought it unhealthy to remain in the vicinity of two such obvious targets and had made off immediately on sighting us.

On coming off watch, Tom and I were anxious above all for some sleep. The decks were heavily crowded but we found a spot on the starboard side of the bow, not far from the ship's gun and were preparing to lie down when a Dutch motor launch came alongside. Its commander had a brief conversation with the captain of our ship and then left. I did not hear what was said.

Figure 6 - Pom Pong Island from the deck of the Tien Kwang. The lifeboat is bringing branches of trees, cut on the island, to camouflage the two ships, Kuala and Tien Kwang

Figure 7 - The gun in the bow of Tien Kwang.
Taken on Saturday 14th February 1942 off Pom Pong Island

Figure 8 - The Kuala off Pom Pong Island
on Saturday 14th February 1942. Taken from the deck of the Tien Kwang

I slept for several hours and when I woke the sun was high in the sky. I got up and looked over the ship's rail towards the island. Some lifeboats had been launched and were bringing branches of trees from the island to camouflage the two ships. This seemed a useless operation. It would have taken a week to cut enough branches to cover the two ships and, furthermore, the Kuala was sending up smoke which even the most perfect camouflage would have had no chance of concealing.

Whether or not it was Kuala's smoke which attracted the attention of the single aircraft which shortly flew over us, I shall never know. The aircraft, however, was clearly a reconnaissance plane since within five minutes of its departure, a group of bombers appeared. In the anxiety of the moment I did not count them, but there were perhaps six or eight, flying in close formation. They first bombed the distant ship, which sank immediately. They then wheeled in a wide arc and straightened on a course which would obviously take them first over Kuala and then over Tien Kwang, though which of us they intended to attack first was not clear.

"Take cover," bellowed a voice of authority, but there was little cover available. I and those around me could only lie face down on the deck, hands clasped over heads, and hope for the best. The noise of the aircraft engines grew rapidly louder. There were a few moments of paralysing suspense then down came the rain of death, a quick series of massive explosions followed by a rattle of bomb splinters hitting our superstructure. Kuala had been the target and when I rose to look at her she was on fire, surrounded by debris and struggling survivors. I remember especially the screams of the women. Men also no doubt cried out but it was the women's voices which carried across the water.

I do not recall seeing the Kuala sink. This was because my attention was diverted by someone on our vessel shouting "They're wheeling!" This meant that an attack on us, the last of the sitting ducks, was inevitable. It took the aircraft perhaps a minute to position themselves for their bombing run and during this time some of the people on the Tien Kwang dived overboard and began swimming for the island. As the planes were clearly about to attack, the order was given "Abandon

Ship!" Then, as I reached the ship's rail, another order was shouted: "Take your shoes off before you go in!" As I did so I remembered that I was wearing a cork life-jacket, the type which, I had heard, could snap a man's neck on impact with the water. I therefore looked over the ship's side to see if, by chance, there was a rope down which I might make a more gentle entry into the water. Incredibly, there was one, and down it I went.

On reaching the water I pushed off from the ship's side and started to swim, but the life jacket was a considerable encumbrance. So were my stockings, which came partly off and trailed behind me. My shirt sleeves also hindered me. On the ship they had been rolled up at the elbow but in the water, they unrolled and added further resistance to my efforts. I managed to get the stockings off and was beginning to make slightly better progress when someone, much to my annoyance, grabbed my legs gasping "Give us a hand. I'm done. " It was a friend of mine, Sergeant Chippendale ("Chips" as he was more familiarly known) and he looked dreadful. His face was pale, his eyes were protruding and he was gasping for breath. I took hold of him under the armpits and started to swim backwards in the manner prescribed for life saving, but it was harder work than I had expected and progress was painfully slow. As, however, we both had life jackets there was no danger of either of us sinking, and this encouraged me. We struggled on and after some minutes Chips was able to use his legs quite effectively again. With two pairs of legs in action we made much better progress and in a few more minutes we were on the boulder strewn beach of the island.

I was anxious to get under the cover of the trees but Chips insisted on resting before attempting to climb up the slope. I therefore left him and went on with others. After a few minutes I paused for breath beside a rotund sailor, to whom I remarked

"I think we've bloody had it."

"Rubbish, mate," he replied. "I've survived two sinkings and I'll bloody well survive this one. First we've got to find water. If we can do that we're made."

I admired his pluck and envied his optimism.

I have no recollection of any bombing either while I was swimming from the ship to the island, or after I landed on the island. This is strange because so many other details of the episode remain so clearly in my mind. That bombs were dropped on us is nevertheless beyond doubt, the resultant casualties among friends of mine bearing certain witness to the fact.

We climbed up to the summit of the island and descended to a sandy beach on the other side. Here we took off our clothes to dry them and it was then I realised I had lost my glasses, but I could not recall the moment of losing them. My wrist watch, which had been a twenty-first birthday present eight months previously, was full of water and had stopped. I now had nothing apart from a khaki drill shirt(with long sleeves), a singlet, a pair of khaki drill shorts and an identity disc on a piece of string. The identity disc, which I had hung by its string on a bush, I overlooked when I put my clothes back on.

Few people seemed to have crossed the island. I doubt if there were more than twenty or thirty of us, but we were shortly joined by a party of survivors from the Kuala who arrived in a lifeboat, having rowed round the island. Some of them were injured. I remember particularly an elderly woman sitting propped against a tree.

"Nurse," she kept saying, "I'm sure my anus has been damaged."

"Nonsense, Sister," replied a young nurse who was with her, "You have only a flesh wound in the buttock." The sister nevertheless, looked very ill. I remember also seeing people trying to dispose of the body of a woman by pushing it out to sea, the long black hair of the woman undulating on the water.

I desperately wanted a cigarette but, not surprisingly, neither I nor any of my friends had any. We were bemoaning this fact when a man, lying on his back some three or four yards away and seeming to be dead, suddenly said "I can give you a fag." We thought he was joking but he produced a round tin of fifty Players and gave us one each. He also produced a box of matches.

"How did you keep the matches dry?" I asked.

"Oh," said the man, "I just held them above my head as I swam." Such coolness seemed to me doubtful and yet how else could he possibly have prevented the matches from becoming soaked?

After an hour or so, some friends and I decided to return to the other side of the island where presumably the majority of the survivors of the two ships had landed and remained. We did so, meeting on the way groups of people of all kinds, servicemen and civilians; men, women and children; British, Chinese, Indians and Eurasians. There were hundreds. We reached the bay in which the two ships had anchored and saw that Tien Kwang was still afloat, though listing heavily. On the beach there were two or three lifeboats from the stricken ships, and a dinghy. From conversations with various friends on this side of the island I gradually pieced together a casualty list of people I knew. Laurie Bowen and Jimmy Dolman, both radar operators, had been killed, Bowen by an abdominal wound, Dolman by bomb blast. One of our cooks and a Corporal Chiltern had also died. Flying Officer Hogg, our station adjutant, had suffered a severe wound near the elbow and seemed likely to lose his arm. Reg Bussey had a head wound and Chippendale a back wound, sustained on the beach after I had left him. Corporal Fairbass, an RAF policeman, was suffering from blast and Percy Toms, also of the RAF police, along with Bill Horne, a radar operator, were missing.

I also learned that a spring had been discovered close to the bay and that arrangements were in hand to issue all survivors with a ration of water twice a day. This was good news since given water, we could survive(as the man had said) for a considerable time, even without food.

During the afternoon an aircraft flew close by but it attacked neither us nor the crippled Tien Kwang. Later in the afternoon towards dusk, volunteers were called for to row out to the Tien Kwang to find food. I was among the volunteers and after a great deal of difficulty we managed to launch one of the lifeboats. Being made of steel, it was extremely heavy and it had been beached when the tide had been at a higher level. We thus had a wide strip of boulder strewn beach to negotiate before reaching the water.

When we reached the ship we were greeted by one of its officers who asked if we had brought the second engineer.

"No," said Flight Lieutenant Connell, who was in charge of us. "We've come to get rations."

"Rations," bawled the ship's officer. "That's typical of the bloody airforce. All they can think of is their bellies. I've been trying to get the bloody pumps going but I need the second engineer to give me a hand."

Connell said he hadn't been aware of this, but if he had been, he would have gladly brought the man. Who was this second engineer anyway, and where was he?

"Christ knows where he is," shouted the naval officer, "It's too late anyway. The ship's done for."

We went aboard and found some tins of bully beef and some ship's biscuits which we lowered into the lifeboat. I also recovered my sidepack from where I had been lying on the deck, but I could not find my shoes. However, there were plenty of shoes lying about and I had no difficulty in finding a pair that fitted. I also picked up a blanket which I later discovered was rather worn, but it was better than nothing. In the sidepack were my camera, some photographs, films and photographic paper, a shirt, a towel a pair of stockings, two tins of maconochie, a radio book, a housewife, a safety razor, an enamel plate, a spoon and some cigarettes. Other members of the party acquired equipment similarly and when we got back in the lifeboat she was loaded to capacity.

We were about to push off when the RN Officer appeared again, angry as ever.

"You can chuck some of that bloody baggage off," he said "I'm coming in that boat with my men."

There was some argument about what should be dumped and in the confusion(or perhaps by design) Flight Lieutenant Connell's huge suitcase, containing among other things his cine camera, disappeared over the side. He was very cross.

With the RN Officer and his men in the lifeboat our freeboard was about three inches and we were in considerable danger of sinking. We had to row, therefore, with the greatest of care. This we did, making first for the boulder covered beach, which was the nearest point of the island. Here we halted in shallow water and disembarked some half a dozen people, myself included, who then waded ashore. The lifeboat, thus lightened and in a safer condition, was then rowed round to the opposite side of the island where the sandy coastline was more suitable for both the beaching and launching of boats.

Several of us who had got out of the lifeboat also made our way over to the sandy beach. It was dark and the beach seemed deserted. We were surprised therefore when we almost tripped over the body of a stout man. He was lying on his back and either dead or asleep. We prodded him and he grunted and stirred.

"Are you alright?" we asked.

"Alright?" he said "Alright?" cynically emphasising the word. "Nobody's alright. We've 'ad it, matey." On further questioning, he turned out to be the Tien Kwang's elusive second engineer. We told him he had been wanted on board to help with the pumps, but we could not convince him that there had ever been any hope for the vessel. There was certainly no hope now and no point in pursuing the conversation, so we left him to his slumber.

Further along the beach we came across a middle-aged couple huddled together in a depression in the sand. The man had malaria and was shivering violently. His wife had given him her cardigan but it was wispy and small and obviously not of much use. The woman asked if we could spare any clothing and I gave her the shirt and stockings from my sidepack.

There seemed nothing now to do but to lie down and sleep, which we did, in a hollow in the sand, about five of us. It was a rough billet but I slept soundly till dawn. On waking, food was our first thought and we accordingly made our way over to the other side of the island where we assumed there would be a distribution of both food and water.

As we descended the slope towards the bay, we saw that the Tien Kwang had disappeared. We saw also that there was oil on the water of the bay and we knew then that the ship had gone down, though whether she had sunk as a result of the damage she sustained, or had been scuttled, we could not tell. There had been talk of scuttling her to remove the risk of further bombing, or unwelcome attentions, by the Japanese, and from that point of view I was glad she had gone, but I was concerned that we now had no obvious means of escape from the island.

The ration was a hard biscuit, about a cubic inch of bully beef and a small measure of water, perhaps a quarter of a pint. The water had to be drunk at the spring unless one had a container. It was a poor breakfast and there was to be no further meal until evening. During the past two or three days my appetite for food had been suppressed by the anxiety to survive, but now that I felt relatively safe again the desire for food began to reassert itself and I was strongly tempted to open the maconochie. Not certain, however, how long we might have to stay on the island, I resisted the temptation and made do with a cigarette.

After breakfast I met my friend McBain, whom I had not seen since abandoning ship. He told me a motor launch had called during the night and evacuated some of the more seriously wounded. This information cheered me to some extent because it meant our predicament was known beyond the confines of the island and further boats, I presumed, would arrive in due course.

I also came across Taffy Jones, the eighteen year old from Lake Vyrnwy whom I had met briefly on the ship.

"Hallo, Taff," I said, "I thought you couldn't swim."

"That's right," he said, "but I can swim now can't I!"

Apart from taking some photographs, I spent the rest of the daylight hours that Sunday making a nominal roll of the survivors. This job I took over from Flying Officer Bellassis. He was a man in his fifties and seemed pleased when I offered to relieve him. The task necessitated touring the island and taking the names of as many people as possible. I tried to cover the island methodically but I doubt if I penetrated every remote corner of it. There was also the difficulty that people were moving about and this no doubt caused some of them to slip through the net. I did not count the number of names collected, but there were some hundreds. Whether the list survived and was ultimately of some value, I never knew.

In the evening the second and last meal of the day was served. It was the same as breakfast and it did no more than whet the appetite. It was precious nevertheless and I ate it slowly, obsessively proportioning each mouthful of the two ingredients to ensure the bully beef was not exhausted before the biscuit.

After the meal, I lay and talked with three or four friends under the trees on the slope of the bay. The cigarettes which I had brought from the ship were a godsend in the absence of food, and we smoked several. It was, in a sense, an idyllic setting, the ceiling of trees gently stirring in the occasional breeze, the sea lapping at the shore and night approaching to complete the peace. Talk was of chances of rescue, and the fate of Singapore. On the matter of rescue we were optimistic, given that food and water, especially the latter, would hold out. Singapore, we were certain, was doomed and we were fearful for its defenders and its inhabitants, especially in view of Japanese depredations and brutalities in China and in other areas which they had overrun.

As darkness deepened, conversation flagged and one by one we began to drift into sleep. Then, it seemed immediately on falling asleep, I became aware of someone asking if anyone could "do Morse". Half asleep, I automatically said I could. Then, suddenly recalling my experience of signalling duties on the ship, I regretted the admission, but it was too late. I found myself all too quickly being conducted down the slope towards the beach.

Figure 9 - Survivors of Kuala & Tien Kwang on Pom Pong Island
On the left, in pensive pose,is AC1 B. Scott, RAF. Next to him, in white vest and shorts is AC1 J Williams, RAF.

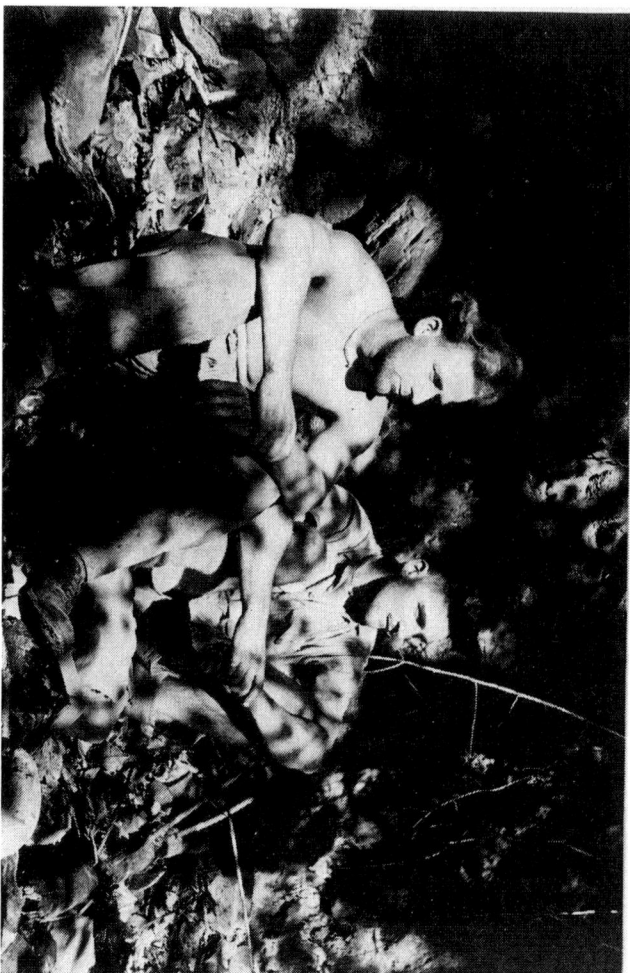

Figure 10 - Two more survivors on Pom Pong Island
Left: LAC H Lander (RAF) Right: LAC E Haynes (RAF)

38

Figure 11 - Camouflaged lifeboat and a group
of survivors on the rock strewn beach of Pom Pong Island.

39

Figure 12 - Some of the wounded on Pom Pong Island (AC1 B Scott, RAF, crouching right foreground)

Figure 13 - Grave of Corporal Fairbass,
RAF Police on Pom Pong Island

At the beach, I was handed over to an army captain.

"I've found you a signalman," said my captor.

"Good show," said the captain, and proceeded to explain my duties. I was to sleep beside him while he kept lookout. If he sighted a ship, he would waken me and I would then signal the ship with the Aldis lamp. He indicated a tattered mattress which was lying near and I lost no time in getting down on it. This was unexpected luxury and I quickly fell asleep, but I woke again just as quickly. The mattress was full of bugs and they were biting me fiercely. I fought them for a while but it was an unequal struggle and I was eventually forced off the mattress. The beach was hard and stony but I was tired and fell into deep sleep without difficulty.

My next recollection is of being roughly shaken by the shoulder and the sound of an excited voice shouting "A ship. A ship. Come on. Wake up. A ship."

I sat up and rubbed my eyes. "Where?" I asked, desperately trying to gather my senses.

"There," said the captain, "Over there. See it?"

I looked in the direction indicated but, being short sighted and without glasses, I saw nothing.

"Quick," he said, "Send a signal," as if the vessel might suddenly evaporate.

"What shall I say?" I asked.

"Just tell them we're survivors of Tien Kwang and Kuala and need help," he replied.

I picked up the lamp and was about to start sending when it occurred to me that the ship might be Japanese. This I felt compelled to mention, if only obliquely, so without lowering the lamp, but glancing sideways at the officer, I said "I presume she's British."

"So do I," replied the captain, which seemed to me that he had weighed the risk and made his decision. I therefore sent the signal approximately in the direction indicated. The message read "SOS SOS de survivors of SS Tien Kwang and Kuala. AR."

We waited some minutes for a reply but none came. The ship, however, did not open fire and this encouraged us.

"Repeat the signal," ordered the captain. I did so, but again there was no response. This baffled me. Surely she had seen our signal, and, if she had, why hadn't she acknowledged? I could only assume that she was not prepared to risk sending even the single letter "R", which would have indicated receipt, for fear of attracting enemy attention. The captain also apparently assumed that the ship had received our message, since he gave no order for any further repetition of the signal.

We now awaited events. The captain looked fixedly at the vessel and I peered hopefully in the same direction. I saw nothing and grew tired of watching. Then suddenly the captain spoke.

"She's moving," he said. "See her?" I squinted hard, but to no avail. "Yes," he added tensely a few moments later. "She's definitely moving." He continued to watch intently for a few more minutes, and then "She's moving in," he shouted. "Quick. We must rouse the dinghy crew. Come on." We set off, trying to run across the rock covered beach but slipping and stumbling at almost every step - I particularly because I was hampered not only by short sight but also my rubber soled shoes which gave no grip on the slippery boulders, many of which had oil on them from the sunken Tien Kwang. The captain held me tightly by the arm to support me and, at every false step I made, encouraged me onward with his regimental battle cry "Steady the Buffs." He was apparently of the Royal East Kent Regiment.

When we reached the dinghy I was instructed to remain by it while the captain went to rouse the crew. When he came back with the crew we launched the boat and I took the tiller, steering in the direction indicated by the captain, which was round the headland at the side of the bay. I had still not seen the vessel, but when we rounded the headland, sure enough, there she was. As we approached, someone on the vessel hailed us through a megaphone and asked us to identify ourselves. We said we were survivors of the Tien Kwang and Kuala, sunk by enemy action the previous day. This seemed to satisfy the commander and a hatch was opened in the vessel's side. We rowed up to it and the army captain went aboard.

While we were waiting for him we talked to some of the crew who told us their ship was the RN sloop, Tanjong Penang. We asked them for food but they were on iron rations and were able to give us only hard tack and a few handfuls of raisins. We ate the meagre fare gratefully enough but it was a disappointment that normal rations were not available. I had visualised bread and butter, and cheese, and steaming wholesome stew with generous quantities of hot sweet tea.

His parley over, our captain returned to the dinghy and we rowed back to the shore. The captain of the sloop had agreed to evacuate survivors and these now had to be ferried from the island. I do not know how many people the Tanjong Penang took aboard, but it was a large number and they were chiefly nurses and civilians. The embarkation was completed in darkness and the ship sailed before the sun rose.

We who were left behind were mainly service personnel and we naturally considered ourselves unlucky, but fate in war is remarkably unpredictable. Some years later, when the war had finished, I learned that the Tanjong Penang had been sunk by enemy action shortly after leaving Pom Pong, and that there had been heavy loss of life.

On the day after the visit of the Tanjong Penang, news began to circulate that Singapore had capitulated on the previous day, Sunday, 15 February. I was surprised that the news had arrived so quickly, we having no radio equipment, but I now assume that the information came from the Tanjong Penang during her call, she apparently having received it either in a news broadcast or in a signal from the Admiralty. Although I was not surprised that Singapore had surrendered, I was deeply saddened by the humiliation of our defeat.

On the same day, I also heard that Corporal Fairbass had died from peritonitis caused by his bomb blast injuries. I was shown his grave at the head of which a rough wooden cross had been planted, and I photographed it.

There now followed several days of uneventful waiting. There was hope that a further ship would be sent, but no certainty, and as the days slipped by my optimism began to waver. I would have been less anxious if there had been something to do but we could only lie about or wander around, and gossip. Most of this period I spent with four or five airforce friends. We discussed everything and nothing. Twice a day we drew our scanty rations, which had not been increased despite the reduced number of people now on the island, and on two occasions I supplemented them with a tin of maconochie. The tinned meat and vegetables were manna compared with the bully beef and biscuits, but as a tin provided each man with only two or three mouthfuls our appetites were more teased than appeased.

The waiting lasted four or five days but a ship did eventually arrive. She was a shabby looking Chinese sailing junk, rather small, perhaps forty feet in length. We went aboard and were directed into the hold, a bare wooden cavity, on the floor of which we sat tightly packed together. We were strictly enjoined not to go on deck during daylight hours, except for purposes of relieving ourselves, and then only with permission. The purpose of this restriction was to preserve the appearance of an innocent native trading vessel in the event of our being observed by any marauding Japanese aircraft. Thus we left Pom Pong, at dusk, creaking our way across the South China Sea in considerable discomfort, but glad to be once again on the move.

Figure 14 - In the hold the of Chinese Junk which evacuated the last of the survivors from Pom Pong Island.

Of the five men in the back row only AC1, F.C.A. McBain (second from left) is positively identifiable, but it is probably LAC A.J. Morris at third from left and Cpl.L.O'Neil (RAF) on the extreme right of the row. AC1, J.A. Blount is in the centre of the photograph, AC1, B.Scott is at the left hand corner, LAC D.J. Cusaek is at the centre of the right hand edge and the head of LAC N.Kelly is just visible in the centre foreground.

46

Chapter Three - Captured in Sumatra

When darkness came, although some people went on deck to sleep, thus giving the rest of us some extra space, it was still very crowded in the hold of the junk and I was not able to stretch out at full length. As I lay there, convoluted in the silence, with my sidepack for a pillow, I remember thinking that I would never sleep. But sleep I did and, when I woke, it was to the confusion of those who had slept on deck being urged below, and those below struggling upwards to relieve themselves. It was dawn and the Chinese captain, a weather-beaten, scrawny little man, was anxious to get everybody below decks.

"Lacass! Lacass!" he kept shouting.

This was the Malay word for "hurry", but it was ten minutes before we were all back in the hold. On deck, it was a fine bright morning and the wind was filling our sail.

An hour or so passed and breakfast arrived. This consisted of boiled rice mixed with bully-beef, and was served from a bucket. Each man received about three spoonfuls. We were also given a single ration of drinking water. It was no feast, but my thoughts were more on safely arriving at our destination than on food.

We did not know where we were going except that it was to a large island off the east coast of Sumatra, and that the voyage was expected to take about a day. Our progress, however, depended on wind and by the middle of the morning there was none. Our vessel consequently came to a graceful but distinct halt. We knew she had stopped because the creaking of her timbers had ceased. I was not at first greatly worried. Indeed the total silence and absence of motion had a pleasantly soporific effect. But as time went by the silence became oppressive and I began to feel anxious.The temperature in the hold rose with the height of the sun and, by afternoon, it was scarcely bearable. Requests for permission to go on deck increased out of all proportion to the limited amount of food and water which had been distributed and the captain of the junk became increasingly agitated as more and more men were allowed out of the hold. His problem, however, was dramatically resolved by the appearance of an aircraft. On seeing this, those on deck needed no more persuasion. They were back in the hold in the twinkling of an eye.

The aircraft was fairly low and as the sound of its engines grew louder there was an apprehensive silence in the hold. People stared stoically ahead or at each other, but the occasional involuntary upward glance betrayed the fear that was in all of us. The aircraft flew directly over us on a straight course and as its deadly sound receded so our conversation and our courage returned.

The second meal of the day was served in the late afternoon and we ate it with zest, not because the menu had in any way improved, ingredients and portions being as before, but because a blessed breeze had at last sprung up and was beginning to propel the ship forward. As the wind rose, so did our spirits, to the point where some of our number felt moved to sing. But the singers were not strongly supported and after a few minutes they abandoned their efforts. I think most of us felt that such an overt demonstration of confidence might once again rouse the fates against us, and we were not prepared to take the risk. But there was an optimistic mood among us and I certainly went to sleep more hopeful.

In the morning my first thought was whether the junk was still moving. She was and, judging from the groaning of her timbers, was making good progress. With breakfast came the message that the captain expected to make port that afternoon, and shortly after noon, we received the further news that our destination was now in sight. This gave me the impression that we were on the point of landing, but in fact it was almost dark when we finally stepped ashore at Dabo on the island of Singkep.

Singkep was indeed a much bigger island than Pom Pong. It was nearer the size of Singapore Island, but more rural and remote, being some thirty miles from the Sumatran mainland. Its most notable feature, from our point of view, was that it was inhabited and therefore promised more reliable supplies of food and water. Nor were we disappointed. Shortly after arriving on the island we were given what seemed to us a generous banquet - boiled rice and thick vegetable stew, both in generous quantity. It was a great pleasure once again to experience a full stomach and a satisfying belch.

On Singkep, we learned that an escape route for Singapore refugees was in operation in Sumatra. The refugees, who were chiefly service men and were landing at various points along the east coast of Sumatra, were being funnelled westward, mainly along the Kampar, Inderagiri and Jambi rivers, to Padang on the west coast, and from there being evacuated by ship. this was welcome news, but we also heard that Japanese parachute troops had occupied Palembang, a major town on the Sumatran mainland about two hundred miles to the south of us. There was therefore risk that the Japanese might either cut us off from Padang if they marched north, or occupy Padang before we could reach it. Not surprisingly, therefore, having spent a night on Singkep, we were anxious to move on. The captain of the junk, however, was unwilling to sail and put forward every possible reason for not doing so. First he said he expected rough weather, then he said tides were unsuitable and finally he insisted on going ashore for victuals. As a result we had to spend a second night on Singkep, but the next day the entreaties of our officers were successful and the captain agreed to sail, though whether it was money or threats which caused him to comply, I never discovered. Perhaps it was a combination of both. The main point was that we were once again on the move, this time bound for the mainland of Sumatra.

Figure 15 - Native houses at Dabo, on Singkep Island

Figure 16 -One of the huts at Dabo, Singkep
in which escapers from Singapore were accommodated

51

Figure 17 - Group at Dabo

Left to right: AC1 TL Bouette, the author, AC1 B Scott,
LAC AP Phillips, AC1 J Williams (all RAF) and a local inhabitant

52

Figure 18 - F/O   EW Smith, Royal Canadian Air Force
Note the footwear, fashioned from crepe rubber sheet

Figure 19 - RAF group at Dabo, Singkep Island

Back row left to right:Unknown, LAC AC Phillips, AC1 AS Vaisey, AC1 FCA McBain, Cpl J Rounding,
AC1 J Williams, F/O EW Smith (RCAF), AC1 S Bracewell, Cpl D Verrells,
AC1 TL Bouttte, AC1 EJ Blakelock, LAC AJ Morris, Cpl O'Neill

Middle Row left to right:
LAC Wardell, unknown, AC1 RT Bussey, LAC H Lander, LAC E Haynes, LAC N Kelly

Front Row left to right:
LAC Jones, AC1 B Scott, Cpl RJ Beatty, AC1 JA Blount, LAC J Barker,
AC1 WH Coglan, Davies (rank & initials not known), LAC D Cremin

54

After a day and night on the junk, we reached the broad mouth of Inderagiri River and were told by one of our number, Stan Vaisey, who had been in conversation with the vessel's captain, that we were close to our destination. Stan did not know the name of the place at which we were going to land but he understood it was the seat of a local rajah. This information intrigued us greatly and, on being solemnly assured by Stan that he was not joking, we fell to speculating eagerly on the delights likely to be heaped upon us by this wealthy potentate. Food and drink, it was widely agreed, would be on a lavish scale. Indeed, there might even be dancing girls. Then reality smote us. the place at which we landed was a small village built on piles driven into the muddy bank of the river, a humble place and clearly not the abode of anyone of note. Its name was Priggi Rajah, and herein lay the cause of the misunderstanding. Stan had mistaken the word "priggi", meaning "well", for "piggi" which means "go". He had thus thought we were going to see a rajah, whereas in fact we were going to a place called "Rajah's Well". Stan's skill in Malay had hitherto been widely acknowledged and admired but, as a result of this unfortunate error, his reputation was reduced.

Why we went to Priggi Rajah I do not know. It was a peculiar place, perched on its stilts above ooze in which strange looking mud fish plopped and slithered like creatures from another planet. We went ashore and bought coconuts, which gave us all diarrhoea, but otherwise achieved nothing. We spent the night on the junk and then again set sail, westward up the Inderagiri River.

Our next port of call was Ayer Muluk, a rubber estate which had been converted to a transit camp for refugees from Singapore. Here we were accommodated in brick built huts which, in normal times, had been used for the processing and packing of rubber. Crepe rubber sheet was everywhere and we used it for bedding. There were also scores of rubber tappers' cups, which those of us who lacked utensils, used as eating and drinking vessels. Food was limited, but regularly distributed twice a day.

Figure 20 - Priggi Rajah
at the mouth of the Inderagiri River

Figure 21 - Covered market at Tembilahan

Figure 22 - Village square, Tembilahan
(with rear view of the banana fritter merchant)

58

Figure 23 - Changing boats in mid-river at Rengat

59

From Ayer Muluk we continued our journey along the Inderageri River in barges, some of which were motor driven and some of which were towed by motor boats. Camps had been established at various places along the river and in some of them we stopped for several days. One of these was Tembilahan and I recall it particularly, not only because we stayed in it for some days, but also because it was here that I was introduced to banana fritters. This delicacy was regularly brought into the camp by an enterprising native who, at a cent a time, did a roaring trade.

The barges in which we travelled were open and bare and often dirty, one of them in particular, which had obviously been recently used for hauling coal. But it was pleasant enough, chugging along the broad, slow moving river between steep banks of dark green jungle, silent except for the occasional screech of unseen monkeys. Now and then, in a clearing on the river bank, a small village would come into view; neat atap huts nestling behind small boats at the water's edge and brown skinned natives waving to us as if we were tourists.

But gradually the river narrowed and grew shallower until at Taluk, our boat journey ended. Taluk was another transit camp and from here we were to be transported by bus. Buses, however, were in short supply and several days went by without a sign of one. Then the rain came and the river, which our bus had to cross by ferry, flooded its banks and inundated the surrounding countryside. Thus marooned, we spent our time gazing at the vast expanse of water and cursing (a) providence for allowing the deluge, and (b) quite unreasonably, the Dutch for failing to get us out of Taluk before the flood. The water was spread over such a wide area that it looked quite permanent. However, after several anxious days, it did subside and our motor bus arrived to take us on the next leg of our journey, which was to Sawaloento, a railhead some fifty miles away in the eastern foothills of the mountain range which lies parallel to the west coast of the country.

Figure 24 - Flooded river at Taluk

61

Figure 25 - A motor bus being ferried across the Inderagiri River at Taluk after the flood had subsided

We reached Sawaloento within the day, and from there we had a luxurious train ride across the mountains and down to Padang on the coast. I have no record of our date of arrival but it was probably the beginning of March.

Padang had paved streets, permanent buildings, shops, attractive suburbs and all the signs of a well run and peaceful little town. It was the most civilised place we had encountered since leaving Singapore and its metropolitan atmosphere restored in me a degree of security and optimism. My optimism was also based on news that a British cruiser, HMS Danae, had called at Padang four days prior to our arrival, had taken off large numbers of refugees and was expected to return. This information was given to me by Sergeant Chippindale who, because of the wound in his back, had been given priority of transport and had arrived in Padang a week or so before I had. He had had the opportunity of leaving on the Danae but had decided to wait for the rest of his unit to arrive - a decision which I admired but which was subsequently to cost him his life.

In Padang, much to my surprise, I also found Percy Toms and Bill Horne, both of whom I assumed killed at Pom Pong. In fact, after jumping from the Tien Kwang, they had clung with others to a life raft and been carried away from the island by currents. Some of their fellow survivors had lost their grip through exhaustion and slipped into the sea. Others had tried unsuccessfully to swim to islands which seemed closer than they in fact were, but Percy and Bill had hung on for almost four days until finally washed up on another island, from which they had been funnelled into the escape route across Sumatra. Both of them seemed well, despite their ordeal, although Bill had some sores on his legs - the result apparently of the long exposure to sea water.

At Padang, the fleeing British forces were housed partly in the Malay school and partly in the Chinese school. I was in the Malay school. We had only the floor for a bed, but the building was sound and waterproof and we were regularly fed by the Dutch authorities. There were also ample supplies of clean water for washing and drinking.

Figure 26 - View of Sawaloento

Figure 27 - View of Sawaloento

Figure 28 - On the train from Sawaloento to Padang

Figure 29 - A halt on the journey from Sawaloento to Padang

67

We had no responsibilities except to keep our billet tidy, and there was no restriction on our movement. Most of us therefore spent much of our time wandering the town, especially the native bazaar, where those of us who still had money could buy fruits and vegetables of all kinds and at cheap prices. A few of our number, however, with more enterprise than the rest, made a point of exploring the European suburbs of the town. Here, many of them struck gold, for not only did they find generous Dutch householders, but also generous(and pliable) Dutch daughters. Thus we waited for our ship. It was expected to arrive in darkness and hope was therefore at its highest each night when we lay down to sleep. But no ships came and as each uneventful night succeeded another our hopes began to sag. For me, the low point came one night when an RAF Catalina flying boat arrived and evacuated some high ranking Army officers and half a dozen Japanese prisoners. This seemed to indicate that sea rescue of the main body of refugees, numbering about a thousand, was now regarded as either very hazardous, or (more probably) impossible and no longer to be attempted. Either way, our future seemed perilous and as the days continued to slip by my anxiety increased. I discussed with McBain the possibility of stealing a small boat and trying to make our way to India, but we came to the conclusion that the odds against us were too high since neither of us knew anything about navigation or seamanship and the distance facing us was so great. We also felt that the Japanese were more likely to despatch out of hand a small party of people intercepted on the open sea than a larger body of troops captured on land. Capture in any circumstances was an ugly prospect, but eventually we had to accept that no other outcome was likely. Too much time had elapsed for there to be any hope of a ship and there was clearly no preparation for any defence of the town. Indeed, the Dutch had impounded the weapons of the British troops on arrival so even individual resistance was out of the question.

While waiting for doomsday, we continued to make our daily trips to the town and during one such expedition I managed to get the film from my camera developed by a Chinese chemist. I paid for this service with the photographic paper I had brought with me from Singapore, thus preserving the few precious dollars I still had left. Then, on another visit to the town, a day or two later, we were surprised by notices in the street which stated that Padang had been declared an open town and would be surrendered to the Japanese army the following morning. The notices also imposed a curfew which required all people to be off the streets from midnight until dawn on the day of the occupation. Thus came the sudden and absolute end of all hope of escape, and I began immediately to think of how the Japanese might treat us. They were undoubtedly an unpredictable race, but I came to the conclusion that as a result of the orderliness of the surrender we had a fair chance of being spared any major brutality. In any event, there was nothing which an individual could do. We were pawns in a huge game of chess over which no-one at my level had the slightest control. This feeling of individual helplessness had grown continuously in me throughout the Far Eastern War, and at Padang, on the eve of our capture, it overwhelmed me. We were now at the centre of the vortex and on the point of being sucked under. We could now only return to our billet and wait for the morning but, before I went back to the Malay school, I bought a pillow, a straw hat and a mat made of rice straw. Inside the pillow I put my negatives enclosed in a small tin box.

When we woke on the morning of surrender, which was 17th March, there was no sign of the Japanese. We had breakfast and there was still no sign of them. Then at about ten o'clock a solitary Japanese soldier took up guard at the end of the lane which led to the school. He was about fifty yards from the entrance to the school and he stood at ease, rifle in hand, with his back towards us. His khaki trousers had green patches on them, one on each buttock.

Later in the day we each had to fill in a form giving name, rank, number, etc, and we were then marched by Japanese soldiers to the nearby Dutch barracks. En route there was some jeering from the natives who lined the streets, but otherwise our journey was uneventful.

At the barracks, we were joined by Dutch soldiers as well as our British comrades from the Chinese school. At the Chinese school the occupation had not been quite as peaceful as had been hoped.

A Japanese officer had been incensed by the sight of a picture of Chiang Kai-Shek and had furiously hacked it to pieces with his sword. We laughed when told of this episode, but privately I was concerned that the Japanese were capable of such primitive violence on such slight provocation.

The barracks were single storied and built on four sides of a rectangle of grass, and between the barracks and the grass there ran a metalled road. There were no furnishings in the barracks and they were therefore rather stark, but they were solidly built, and cool. Shade was also available on the central grass plot, where there were several trees. The barrack windows, which faced outwards towards the town, were all vertically barred and this was a constant reminder that we were now prisoners, but otherwise I thought the accommodation surprisingly good.

Food was regularly supplied and consisted mainly of bread and soup. The ration, however, was small and we became very hungry, unlike our Dutch allies who obviously had plenty to eat. I never discovered for certain why this was so but I presume that, being on home ground, the Dutch were able to make private arrangements for the supplementation of their diet, whereas we were totally dependant on the Japanese. But whatever the cause of the disparity in the rations, the fact was that we were hungry and the Dutch were not. One or two of my more cunning confreres managed to build a relationship with the Dutch and to wheedle food from them, but efforts which I made to inveigle the Dutch, came to nothing. The Dutch, however, were not the only possible source of extra rations. An enterprising group of British prisoners captured a hen by means of a bent pin on the end of a piece of string. This crude device, baited I presume, was lowered through one of the barred windows which gave onto the outside world and, hey presto, chicken stew. I saw the bird landed but I was not invited to join in the feast.

The Japanese at Padang barracks kept a remarkably low profile. A single guard, who was relieved every few hours, represented the only obvious presence of the enemy. We had to bow to him when we met him and there was one guard who took particular delight in wakening, and demanding a bow from, any prisoner he found asleep, but otherwise we were not molested. Occasionally the Japanese took a small party of prisoners to work at the docks but most of us, including myself, never had to work. The boredom was slightly relieved by the organisation of classes in various subjects and I went to Spanish class, but this occupied no more than two hours a day and the remainder of the time was spent aimlessly talking and sleeping. However, not all my talking time was wasted. I happened to mention to Flying Officer Smith of the Royal Canadian Airforce, who had been my last commanding officer in Malaya, that I had lost my glasses during the Pom Pong episode, and he said he thought he might be able to get me a new pair. Money was available from what he called "Battalion Funds" and the Japanese might be persuaded to let me visit a local optician. I thought this extremely unlikely but, shortly afterwards, I was told that arrangements had been made and I was duly taken by a diminutive Japanese soldier to an optician in the town. The optician was a corpulent German and, after testing my eyes, he said my glasses would be sent to the barracks in the course of the next few days. Before returning to the barracks I was bought an iced drink by my Japanese guard and sure enough, some three or four days later, my glasses duly arrived. They were horn rimmed and very effectively restored my long distance vision.

We stayed at Padang until early May when five hundred of us, including twenty officers, were detailed to move to an undisclosed destination. On the morning of the move we were paraded and counted, given a small loaf of bread and a banana each and marched off by a guard of about twenty-five Japanese soldiers. In addition to their small arms, the Japanese had a machine gun which was carried by four of their number and when I saw this weapon it crossed my mind that they might be intending to dispose of us. However, I felt reassured by the bread and the bananas, since it seemed unlikely the Japanese would have given us these if they had intended to shoot us. On the other hand I then thought, the Japanese were a cunning race and they might well have distributed the rations expressly to induce a false sense of security. I still felt, therefore, rather uneasy as we marched out of the barracks, and I wondered if any of my comrades shared my misgiving, but I didn't enquire.

We were taken to the railway station and here we were again counted. During this process an Australian army medical officer, Lieutenant Colonel Coates, fell foul of one of the guards and was fiercely slapped around the face. This was the first instance of serious violence by the Japanese which I had witnessed and I found it extremely disturbing, especially as Colonel Coates was an elderly man well in his fifties. The slapping went on for some minutes, accompanied by an increasing amount of frenzied shouting by the guard who, I was afraid, was going to lose control completely, but the screaming and the slapping eventually subsided and the guard went away mumbling and scowling like a sulky child. What Colonel Coates did to merit this treatment I never found out.

Shortly after this episode another guard gave me the dregs of an iced fruit drink which he had bought and largely consumed. The glass, when handed to me, contained little more than the remains of two ice cubes and I didn't know whether the gift was intended as a kindness or an insult. However, I took it and said "thank you".

After a long wait in the hot sun, we were relieved when the train eventually arrived. It was similar to the one which had brought us to Padang some two months earlier - a steam engine with passenger coaches. It was a slow journey, the gradient being chiefly upwards, but it was pleasant enough. We were sheltered from the sun, the movement provided breeze and most of the country through which we passed was verdant jungle. Our destination, which we reached at the end of the afternoon, was Fort de Kock, a mountain town about a hundred miles to the north of Padang. On our arrival here we were again counted and then marched into the town. Several of the houses which we passed displayed large red and black swastika flags. These were apparently the homes of Germans whom the Japanese, on occupying the town, had released from internment. The Germans stood at their doorways and on their balconies staring impassively at us as we went by, and I wondered what their thoughts were. Despite the swastika flags, it seemed to me unnatural and unreal that this European nation had allied itself to the Japanese against us.

We spent the night at Fort de Kock in a convent which had been emptied of its customary inhabitants. It was bare of furnishings and we slept on the floor, but we had an ample meal of rice and vegetable stew in the evening and some rice porridge the following morning before resuming our journey.

At Fort de Kock the railway ended. The rest of our trek was therefore by road, in a long convoy of open lorries, with one Japanese guard per lorry. Our direction was northward and we were on the road for some three or four days. Each night we were housed in a village building, often the school, and we were given two meals a day - one in the evening and one in the morning. The weather was hot and dry and the roads were rough and dusty. For much of the way we were hemmed in by deep jungle, but there were some clearer stretches and I recall particularly passing beside the vast expanse of Lake Toba.

The country was very thinly populated. Settlements were small and there were large distances between them. One morning, however, we came to a rather larger place than usual and were greeted by natives, many of them children, on both sides of the road waving Japanese flags and shouting abuse at us. I don't know what they were saying as I didn't understand the language, but there was no mistaking their hostility, especially as several of them were making throat cutting motions with the index finger. I presume that the Japanese arranged this show since the people would have been unlikely to turn out in such numbers, and with so many flags, if they had not been pre-warned of our approach and organised accordingly.

On this journey through northern Sumatra I came across, for the first time in my experience, the word "Indonesia". It was chiefly to be seen chalked on the doors of houses, but at the time I did not understand either its meaning or significance.

Our road journey ended at Belawan Deli, which is the port town serving Medan. Here we were put in an internment camp mainly occupied by Dutch civilians. We spent two or three days in this camp and were then transferred to a small cargo vessel, ironically named the England Maru. Our accommodation on the ship consisted of shelves built along the four walls of the square cargo hold. We were extremely crowded on the shelves and I therefore moved my pitch to the floor of the hold where, although it was dirty, there was more room.

On the day after we went a board the England Maru two further ships arrived, carrying Australian prisoners of war. The three ships then set sail together, northward up the Strait of Malacca. It was an uncomfortable journey. The hold was hot and airless; we were seldom allowed on deck; the food - rice and thin vegetable soup - was inadequate; there were no washing facilities, and at night rats ran about the floor of the hold.

After a day or two in these conditions, Stan Vaisey developed crippling abdominal pains which many of us thought were caused by appendicitis, a serious affliction in the absence of surgical facilities. The MO however(Colonel Coates) diagnosed salt deficiency caused by excessive sweating, and the remedy he prescribed was very simple - a handful of salt. This was duly administered and the effect was dramatic. In half an hour Stan had recovered completely - a remarkable example of the value of professional advice.

At Victoria Point, in the extreme south of Lower Burma, the convoy halted and some of the Australian prisoners were taken ashore. The ships then continued to Mergui, some two hundred miles further north, and here the rest of us disembarked.

74

Chapter Four - Early Days in Burma

At Mergui we were housed in what had been a local school. It was brick built but far too small for the five hundred British and one thousand Australian prisoners who were squeezed into it. The crowding was especially inconvenient at night if one had to go to the latrines, which were outside. We slept on the floor and every square inch was occupied. In the darkness it was therefore impossible to get to the door without falling over somebody and causing great wrath.

Food at Mergui was also poor. For breakfast we were given rice porridge, supplemented on Sundays with a teaspoonful of sugar and at midday and in the evening we had rice with soup made chiefly from a weed-like green vegetable which I couldn't identify. The rice supplied for the midday and evening meals was brown, tasted sour and was full of rat droppings.

In addition to poor food and inadequate housing, we had another problem at Mergui. This was dysentery. There had been isolated cases of the disease on board the ships which had brought us from Sumatra but at Mergui the incidence increased, and in June the first deaths occurred.

We were required to work at Mergui, repairing and extending the nearby airstrip, but after only a day or two of this work I fell sick with dysentery. The onset of the disease was sudden and violent. It started at about midnight and within a couple of hours the bowel motions had become so frequent, and it had become so difficult to pick my way safely among the sleeping forms, that I decided to stay on the latrine, which I did for the rest of the night. The next morning, which was a Sunday, I reported sick and in the afternoon was carried on a stretcher, with my bed roll and sidepack into the hospital.

The hospital was a wooden structure built on stilts and the ward in which I was put had twelve beds in it, six down each side. There were no sheets, blankets or pillows but I had a rice mat which I laid on the bed springs, a blanket to cover me and a pillow for my head. I was thus comparatively comfortable and certainly luckier than some of the later arrivals who had to lie on the floor, all beds having been taken.

At the end of the ward was a row of chairs each with its seat removed and a four gallon petrol can beneath it. These were the commodes and there was a constant procession to and from them, day and night. There were not enough of these commodes. Queues consequently formed and accidents occurred.

I desperately wanted to sleep and could easily have done so, despite the pain in my bowels, but the urge to defecate came too frequently and I kept having to make the weary pilgrimage to the end of the ward, which I didn't always reach without mishap.

In this hospital I heard the death rattle for the first time. It happened in the middle of the night and the victim was an Australian in one of the corner beds. He was elderly and I never knew his name. The rattle went on fitfully for two or three hours and he died before dawn. At breakfast time they carried him out and one of the floor patients was given his bed.

Medicines in the hospital were primitive - a liquid produced from mangosteen skins, and charcoal made by burning rice. Morphia was also available but not in any quantity and it was therefore rarely prescribed. We were visited daily by an Australian army medical officer named Captain Cumming whom I particularly remember for his excellent bedside manner. He listened at length to every patient who wanted to talk, including Leading Seaman Edwards (RN), who was in the next bed to me. L. S. Edwards(or Bungy as he was more intimately known) was delirious, and every morning he had the same message for the MO. In answer to the enquiry "How are we today Edwards?" the reply was always "Don't worry about me, Doctor. I shall be dead by tomorrow. I nearly died last night. I was going down the long dark tunnel and the bells were ringing but then I came out again into the light. Tomorrow, though, I shall die and you won't have to worry about me."

"Oh, you mustn't talk like that," the MO would say "I'm quite sure you'll recover."

76

I doubt if the MO really thought that Bungy would recover, but in fact he did. This, to me, was a miracle, especially as, when he began to recover, it was discovered that his bedding was full of maggot infested excrement.

In the bed on the other side was a young Australian named Carley. He very quickly reached the stage of being unable to get out of bed and as a result he kept fouling the rice sacks which he was using as bedding. The orderlies cleaned him as often as they could, but with no change of bedding available their task was impossible. At night her received less attention than in the day and at dawn his condition was therefore always at its worst. Often, when the sun came up, he would be uncovered, and the sight and the smell of him would nauseate me. He lived for only a few days.

Compared with many cases in the hospital, I preserved a fairly clean condition. I occasionally left my mark en route to the commodes, but so did others. I was therefore surprised when, one morning, Colonel Coates appeared at my bedside and upbraided me for "dirty practices". The inference was that the "dirty practices" were wilfully committed, a view to which I very strongly objected, and said so. I drew attention particularly to the extremely primitive arrangements and said I felt that in such circumstances occasional accidents were inevitable. He said they were not; they were controllable and they must stop. We had a very angry exchange of words for some minutes but he remained totally unreasonable, so I turned over in the bed and said no more. He made a few remarks to the back of my head, which was now facing him, and then went.

After some days in the hospital, including my twenty-second birthday, which fell on 10th June, I felt totally exhausted and craved for sleep. I therefore put it to the captain when he came round one morning, that a shot of morphia would be a good thing. He said (as I knew he would) that his supply of the drug was so limited that he had to reserve it for the most serious cases. I said I thought my case was pretty serious and that, even if I wasn't yet at death's door, I soon would be if I didn't get some sleep. But he was not to be convinced. However, I persisted in my request every morning when he made his rounds, and eventually he agreed to let me have one shot. The injection was given that evening and I slept like a log until well after dawn the following morning. On wakening, I felt greatly refreshed and I said to myself "This is the turning point; I am now going to recover." Then I became aware of a great wetness and I found I was lying in a huge pool of excrement. This temporarily reduced my confidence, but an orderly washed and dried my mat and blanket for me and this restored my optimism.

After the big sleep, I did improve. My trips to the end of the ward grew less frequent and as I began to take more food I felt my energy returning. Three of my friends, however, who were brought into the dysentery ward while I was there, all died. Aircraftman Scott, a fellow radar mechanic, was the first. He died suddenly, only a day or two after being admitted. Then, about a fortnight later, Sgt Chippindale was brought in and died similarly quickly. The third victim, LAC Haynes, one of our cooks, died on the same day as Chippindale, but he had been in the hospital much longer. He became depressed, declined to eat and made an unsuccessful attempt to commit suicide by cutting his throat with a razor blade. After having his throat wound attended to, he was put in a side ward where I visited him on several occasions. He was delirious most of the time and eventually contracted pneumonia, which proved fatal.

When Chips died his gold ring was given to me for safe keeping and at the end of the war I took it back to his parents. They lived at Guisely, in Yorkshire, and I spent a weekend with them. Chips had been their only child and I was therefore expecting uncontrolled grief, but the couple displayed remarkable fortitude and not a tear was shed in my presence. Mrs Chippindale's composure was the result of having recently been converted to Spiritualism which, she was convinced, would shortly produce contact with her lost son. Mr Chippindale's brave front I can only attribute to Yorkshire grit.

Whilst in the dysentery ward, we were told we could write a letter home. This was wonderful news. We had to provide our own writing materials, however, and this proved a problem for many of us. I had only some rough quality toilet paper, but I wrote my letter nevertheless. Most of us also lacked envelopes but we were told that it was necessary only to fold the letters and address them on the outside. This we did and hopefully handed them in. But they were never dispatched. They were found some weeks afterwards thrown into a monsoon drain. I suppose we were stupid to hope that these letters would ever reach home, but drowning men grasp at straws.

When I was well enough I was moved to a smaller ward which was detached from the main hospital building. Here there were about half a dozen of us, all at about the same stage of recovery. Our faces were gaunt and our bodies skeleton thin but we had survived the more obscene stages of the disease and our bowels, though still tender, were largely under control. We were therefore a hopeful and cheerful band.

Each morning in the convalescent ward, I was given two enemas. The first was soap and the second(I believe) silver nitrate. These enemas were a long and unpleasant performance. They were followed, however, by a dose of yeast which I greatly enjoyed. The yeast was somehow made from rice, and came in a milky liquid form, about a wineglass full at a time. Its taste was pleasant and it had an inebriating effect which generally sent me to sleep. I therefore liked it and looked forward to the daily ration which, I am happy to say, continued to be given long after the enema treatment had ceased.

It was in the convalescent ward that I became involved in the peculiar practice of composing menus of delectable food. When the game first started the menu would cover a day's eating. Later it was extended to cover a week, the art being to avoid repetition. I wasn't too fond of this pastime but several of my comrades were heavily addicted and spent hours discussing the relative merits of all kind of exotic dishes. The reason for their masochistic behaviour was obviously the poverty and monotony of our everlasting rice and stew diet but it gave me no pleasure to make endless lists of unobtainable foodstuffs and I regularly resolved not to be drawn in. However, surrounded as I was by so much gastronomic enthusiasm, it was difficult to remain entirely remote from the proceedings.

It was strictly forbidden to go outside the hospital grounds, on pain of death by shooting. Several inmates of the hospital had, nevertheless, gone over the wire at night without being detected, and been hospitably received by the Burmese who had houses nearby. A group of us in the convalescent ward were therefore tempted to make such an expedition and we spent some time discussing the possibility. Three of us eventually decided to take the risk and, an hour or two after darkness fell, we crept stealthily through the perimeter fence which, being constructed only of posts and wire, offered no serious obstacle. We approached one of the houses where lights were burning and where people were sitting in the garden. The occupants spoke some English and ushered us quickly inside. They obviously knew what we were and where we had come from(no doubt having already entertained some of our fellow prisoners) and they lost no time in offering us a meal. We gladly accepted this offer and the meal arrived within minutes. It was a curry and, in view of the condition of my bowels, I hesitated, but I had not had a substantial meal for such a long time, and the smell of the food was so appetising, that I could not resist it. It was delicious, full of meat and succulent vegetables and accompanied by expertly cooked rice in unlimited quantity. We thanked our hosts profusely, and I thought how remarkable it was that these people whose country we had colonised should treat us so generously and with such disregard for their own safety, for if the Japanese had discovered us there is no doubt that the Burmese would at least have been violently beaten.

Before we left, one of the Burmese gave me a bottle of Dr Collis Brown's Chlorodyne, which, the donor assured me, was remarkably effective in the treatment of dysentery. I therefore resolved to reserve this potion for use in extreme emergency. Indeed, I so valued the Chlorodyne that, although I subsequently suffered several severe bouts of dysentery, I never succumbed to the temptation to use it. It thus remained a continual comfort to me throughout my captivity and it was not until after the war that I discovered the negligible value of this nineteenth century patent medicine.

On the day after the nocturnal sortie I suffered the expected relapse and for a period of twenty-four hours paid more than the usual number of visits to the country-style twin seater privy which stood in the grounds. Enthroned there during one of these visits, I was surprised to be joined by Colonel Coates and, as we sat together, grunting fitfully, we had a most friendly conversation. I don't know whether he had forgotten our recent altercation or whether he positively wanted to repair the breach, but at all events we had a most civil exchange, during which it transpired that he had first contracted dysentery himself as an army medical orderly at Gallipoli in 1915. He didn't actually say that he now had dysentery again but, judging from his squishy performance, I think he probably had. Our meeting ended with the gift by him of a generous quantity of Japanese officers' toilet paper. Most of this I did not devote to the job in hand but kept for subsequent use as cigarette paper, which had become a rare commodity.

Shortly after this an event occurred which brought a dramatic end to all thoughts of further excursion from the hospital. This was the death of Schubert. Schubert was an Australian prisoner who had made a habit of going over the wire to sell clothes(on commission). The Japanese had let him off with a caution on the first occasion when they had caught him, but on the second occasion they shot him. This was a dreadful warning which none of us could afford to ignore.

One other event occurred at Mergui hospital which is perhaps worth recording. This was a conversation which I had with Ginger Eccleston. Ginger, who came from Stafford, was an RAF medical orderly at the hospital and had given me the life-saving injection of morphia. He now revealed, much to my astonishment, that the substance injected had in fact been plain water.

My period at Mergui hospital came to an end at the beginning of August, when the Japanese decided to move all prisoners who were fit to travel, to a new camp. Inmates of the hospital had the choice either of moving with the main body of prisoners, or remaining behind and being taken to the new site later. I was inclined at first to opt for staying at the hospital. My bowels were still unreliable, I was thin and weak and it was the season of monsoon rains. Travel was therefore not an attractive proposition. I then thought that if I remained behind in a small group the

Japanese might take the opportunity of liquidating us. I therefore decided to move with the main body of prisoners.

The first stage of the journey was back to the main camp. This, however, was no longer the school. It was a group of newly built huts on a different site. Each hut was about fifty yards long and five yards wide, and consisted of a bamboo framework onto which overlapping pieces of atap were tied to form three walls and a peaked roof. One of the longer sides was left open and, inside the hut, running the full length of the covered side was a bamboo platform some two feet high and eight feet wide. On the platform, feet facing the open side of the hut, each prisoner had a bed space about a yard in width. It was crude accommodation, the type built and lived in by the poorest of the Burmese people but, at least when new, it provided basic protection from the elements.

Our journey from the hospital to the new Mergui campsite took about an hour. We encountered some rain on the way and by the time we reached our destination I was exhausted and had soiled the tail of my shirt. My first job was therefore to wash the shirt and hang it out to dry. This I did, and then lay down to sleep. On waking I went to fetch the shirt but it had gone. I thought at first it might have been blown from the line, but it was nowhere in the area and I eventually came to the reluctant conclusion that it had been stolen. This was a dreadful blow. I now had nothing to cover the upper part of my body except a cotton singlet.

I spent only a day or two at the new Mergui camp. We were then all marched down to the docks and put aboard a small cargo vessel. It was evening and dark, but the weather was fine and we had the option of travelling either in the hold or on the deck. I opted for the deck, firstly because the latrines were there, and secondly because I considered that if we were attacked and sunk I would have a better chance of getting off the vessel than if I had to scramble up the vertical ladder from the hold.

We sailed at about midnight and, for an hour or two, all went well. The sea was calm and the ship slid smoothly along producing just sufficient breeze to make the warm night comfortable. Then, very suddenly, a gale sprang up. Fierce wind, torrential rain and huge waves which caused the ship to plunge and roll in the most alarming manner. Wearing only a singlet and shorts, I was drenched in minutes, and frozen to the marrow, my skin blue and goose pimpled. I tried to get into the hold but there were too many with the same objective and I didn't even reach the top of the ladder. I therefore had to remain on the deck, sheltering as best I could abaft the ship's superstructure. Here I was able to avoid most of the wind but much of the rain continued to find its mark and I remained wet and cold, shivering uncontrollably. This, it seemed, was total misery. But worse was to come. I was seized by the dreaded urge. I struggled against it, clamping my soggy buttocks as tightly together as the shivering would allow, but I hadn't a chance. The force against me was irresistible and I quickly realised I had to get to the latrines. These were wooden boxes, about a yard square and perhaps two and half feet in depth, open at the top and lashed to the seaward side of the ship's rail. I had thought, even before the hurricane, that these contraptions were hardly safe and now, in the storm, as they dipped and soared with the violent motion of the vessel, they looked positively dangerous. But I had to use them; there was no alternative. I therefore stepped reluctantly from my shelter into the driving wind and rain and made my unsteady way across the heaving deck towards the rail. On reaching it, the act of raising my leg to step into the box very nearly undid me and I had another close shave as I struggled to lower my sodden shorts. This had to be accomplished with one hand because I needed the other to hold onto the side of the heaving box. It was thus with much relief that I finally achieved, without mishap, the necessary crouching position above the hole in the bottom of the box. It was a perilous perch. The transverse rolling motion was hair raising, especially on the descending arc when, it seemed the box would surely strike the waves. It never did but the seawater, which from time to time sprayed up though the hole in the floor, was a constant reminder of the insecurity of my position. I consequently lost no time in completing my mission and clambering out of the swinging privy back to the comparative safety of the ship's deck.

By dawn the worst of the hurricane had passed. The waves had subsided and the ship was once again on an even keel. The sun came up and I was grateful for its warmth. It also dried my clothes and I began to feel once again that life was worth living. During the morning we were given a loaf of bread. Much of this bread, including mine, was damp and mouldy but I was hungry and I ate it, mould and all. It then occurred to me that now was the time to get down in the hold, while a proportion of its nocturnal occupants, attracted by the sun, were on deck. There was still, I reminded myself, the danger of being unable to get out of the hold if the ship were attacked, and also the problem of getting to the latrines but I decided that, in view of the misery of the previous night, I would risk these perils and I accordingly made my way down the vertical ladder. The hold was still quite crowded and I had to make do with a position too far from the foot of the ladder for peace of mind, but I was comfortable enough, seated on my bedroll and with my back against a bulkhead.

The weather remained calm and for an hour or two all went well but then, quite suddenly, the dreaded urge returned and I knew I had to get to the latrines. It was hazardous enough stepping over and round people in the hold in order to get to the foot of the ladder in a continent state, but the ladder was the greatest peril. I could have managed if I had not had to bend my legs, but ladder climbing involves a considerable movement of both knee and hip, and the hip movements I found particularly dangerous in relation to my condition. I tried very hard to contain myself but, about halfway up the ladder, the floodgates opened. Most of the output was fortunately retained by my shorts. Ordinary Seaman Gutteridge, however, whose pitch was immediately below the ladder, suffered spray damage and swore at me. I was extremely embarrassed and would like to have commiserated at length, but I could not afford to linger. I therefore tendered a brief apology and continued my upward climb.

My experience in the box on this occasion was less frightening than previously. The sea was comparatively calm and the weather, though dull, was fine, but I had the problem of the soiled shorts. These I could not effectively clean because there was no water.

I did not relish returning to the hold and Gutteridge's wrath but, since my bedroll was still down there, I had no alternative. I therefore re-entered the hold with some trepidation. "Guts", however, who by now had cleaned up the mess, showed no desire to re-open the issue. Indeed, he was remarkably civil, which was a great relief to me. This was probably because I knew him slightly. He came from Walsall and was a survivor from either the Prince of Wales or the Repulse.

We reached our destination, which was Tavoy, in the middle of the night. It was raining when we disembarked and we had a wet march of some two or three miles to the prison camp. This consisted of a group of timber built huts with corrugated roofs. When I arrived at the camp, completely soaked, I removed my waterlogged shoes and peeled off my clinging vest and shorts. I had no change of clothing, but I looked forward to the comfort of at least my blanket and pillow which were rolled inside my straw mat. But alas, the rain had penetrated the mat and wet my blanket. Only the pillow, which had been at the centre of the bedroll was dry enough to be used. I therefore had to lie naked on the floorboards with just the pillow and I quickly fell into a deep sleep.

On waking, at dawn, I found myself once again lying in a pool of excrement. This I discovered when, still only half awake, I turned onto my back and felt the cold wetness strike my buttocks. Then the stench hit my nostrils, destroying the last vestiges of hope. My plight alone was humiliating enough but I was further embarrassed by obscenely expressed complaints from several of my fellow prisoners. Their offensive comments cut me to the quick and angered me beyond measure. They hadn't yet suffered dysentery themselves and they hadn't the intelligence to imagine its appalling effects, but this gap in their experience, I fervently hoped, might shortly be remedied.

At Tavoy, the majority of the prisoners were employed on making an airstrip outside the town, but a second smaller working party was also taken each day into the town to clear up war damage. Of these two parties, the "Town Party" quickly became by far the more popular. This was because it was found to provide easy opportunity for scrounging food and tobacco from the remarkably generous Burmese townsfolk.

Indeed, so great was the popularity of the town party, that rosters had to be drawn up to ensure that each man had his turn.

It was a week or two before I became eligible for the town party and I meanwhile went each day with the main body of prisoners to the airstrip. Here we spent our time chiefly uprooting small trees and scrub and levelling the ground. We used spades, picks and chunkels and we carried the soil in those shovel shaped wicker baskets which are the universal earth moving instrument of the East. Some foraging, however, was found to be possible, even on the airstrip. This took place during the midday break when we were given a meal of rice and stew, which we were allowed to eat in the shade of the trees which surrounded the airstrip. Thanks to the cover afforded by these trees, it was a simple matter to slip away to the nearby village where there was a Buddhist temple. Here, the saffron robed priests dispensed excellent food in the shape of meats and vegetables in various sauces and beautifully cooked white rice in unlimited quantity. But these lunchtime sallies became too popular. Too high a proportion of the workforce disappeared each day and the Japanese inevitably noticed this. They caught half a dozen prisoners in the village and marched them ceremoniously back to the work site. Here the miscreants were made to stand to attention while the Japanese slapped and punched their faces and worked themselves into a torrent of abuse, especially if any prisoner tried to defend himself. They then announced that, in future, all men would eat their midday meal on the airstrip and that, if anyone went into the trees without permission, he would be shot. Thus ended our lunchtime excursions from the Tavoy airstrip.

On the day my turn for the town party came round, it was raining. However, I was now better equipped against the weather, having acquired a rice sack which I draped over my shoulders and secured with a piece of wire at the throat. My outfit thus now consisted of cotton singlet and khaki drill shorts, rice sack cape, brown leather rubber soled shoes and a straw hat. I also carried my sidepack(empty except for an enamel plate and spoon) and slung from it, a small wire handled tin can. There were perhaps a hundred of us in the party and we were marched off four abreast. We had three Japanese guards - two privates and one of more senior rank. The senior man was a cheerful character and remarkably well turned out in shiny brown leather top boots. On his right side was slung a large rectangular map case, also in brown leather, and on his left side there hung a long ceremonial sword in leather scabbard. I was not certain of his rank but I imagine he must have been at least a warrant officer. He marched in front of the party in jaunty fashion, occasionally bursting into song and at the same time waving his drawn sword. The two privates, who by comparison were remarkably morose, marched one on each flank of the column, rifles at the slope.

As we entered the town the open fronted shops on either side of the road exerted a magnetic effect on the column, gradually causing it to divide lengthwise. Only in the middle of the column, where the Japanese privates were stationed, was close order maintained. It was not long, however, before the two guards noticed the divergence and began to register displeasure. "Nanda," they murmured several times. I never found out exactly what this word meant but, judging from the fact that it was always said in a restrained, rather hurt, tone of voice, I knew it was only a mild sort of rebuke, equivalent perhaps to "stupid boy" or "silly fellow". It often therefore had little effect, as in this case, especially as I doubt if anyone more than a yard or two away could have heard it. It was, however, a warning and was generally followed by more vociferous expressions, often accompanied by action. And so it was on the march into Tavoy. The two guards began to go up and down the column threatening the prisoners with their rifle butts and shouting "kurra", "bageero" and "kuneero". The meanings of these words I similarly never found out but the violent way in which they were said, plus the accompanying physical acts, or threat of them, left me in no doubt that they were expressions of extreme displeasure.

The exertions of the two guards did straighten the column to some extent but they got no support from the officer out front. He occasionally glanced behind but was clearly not prepared to give any assistance, and I think this greatly discouraged the two privates. It certainly encouraged us and, except when the guards were very close, we took full advantage of all offers made by the generous shopkeeepers.

I collected boiled eggs, bananas and cheroots, all of which I safely, and gratefully, stowed in my sidepack.

In the town, we were taken to a building which had been damaged by either shells or bombs and our task was to load fallen masonry and other debris into lorries. It was rough unpleasant work, especially in the rain, but I took comfort from the fact that at lunchtime, with luck, there would be opportunity for further foraging, this time in the nearby market hall.

At midday the usual ration arrived - rice and a thin stew. After everyone had been served once it was the custom to line up immediately for any second helping that might be available. The British prisoners called these second helpings "leggies" - a corruption of the Malay word "lagi", meaning "more" - and I normally joined the "leggy queue" along with the rest, but on this occasion I contented myself with the basic ration, which I ate as quickly as possible before making a beeline for the market hall. It was easy enough to slip away, all attention, including that of the Japanese guard, being concentrated on food and shelter from the rain, which was still falling heavily.

On the way to the nearby market hall, while jumping across a monsoon drain, I slipped and fell over, gashing my shin on the concrete rim of the drain. I picked myself up and carried on running but, by the time I reached the covered market, the rain had spread the blood from the injury in the middle of my shin down to my foot. This aroused immediate and widespread sympathy from the stall-holders, most whom were women. They clustered round me and, after many expressions of concern and compassion, they brought a bowl of water and began washing my leg. Then three of them in succession each applied a different powder to the injury. Whether this was a single treatment involving three medicaments, or three treatments arising from different opinions, I never knew. Nor did I discover what the powders were, but I strongly suspect that they were various curry mixtures, since they had a burning effect which considerably intensified the pain of the wound. This rather worried me but compensation swiftly followed in the shape of sugar, tobacco, limes and other valuable commodities which the

Burmese ladies now showered on me from all sides. My sidepack was quickly filled to capacity and, as I left the market hall, I wondered again at the generosity of these people.

It was clear when I rejoined the working party that my absence had not been noticed and this was a considerable relief. It rained for the rest of the day, making the work dismal and muddy, and my shin remained painful, but I considered the bag of goodies ample recompense for these discomforts.

On our way back to the camp at the end of the day, the shopkeepers were again generous but I accepted nothing because my bag was full and I felt that to have carried goods unconcealed might well have provoked the guards.

After the town outing, I spent two or three miserable days working on the airstrip. The weather was continually wet and my leg grew increasingly inflamed and painful. I bathed the leg every evening in warm water, but the wound deteriorated and turned into a tropical ulcer, crimson lipped and purulent, so I reported sick. The MO declared me unfit for work and I spent the next few weeks in camp receiving daily treatment for the ulcer. The treatment consisted of cleaning the ulcer by bathing and scraping, and application of a lint dressing, which was changed each day. I was also given a bandage to keep the lint in place

The healing process was extremely slow, and there were days when I felt the ulcer would never stop suppurating. But I had the comfort of not having to go out to work in the rain which was now incessant. I particularly recall the ceaseless rain because of the noise it made on the corrugated iron roof of the building in which we were housed.

Twice while I was on the sick list the Japanese carried out what we called a sick purge. These occurred when the number of prisoners available for work did not come up to expectation. A couple of Japanese would storm through the huts and, on the basis of nothing more than a cursory visual inspection, detail sick men to join the working party. On the first occasion, the purge did not reach my hut, and on the second, although I was looked at, I was not detailed. This was probably because, in addition to the leg injury, I was also extremely thin as a result of the recent dysentery.

When the ulcer healed, I again went out to work at the airstrip, but not for long. Towards the end of October, the Japanese took us on a third cruise, this time to Moulmein, some two hundred miles further up the Burma coast. We spent less than a day in this town, so I saw very little of it, but I remember its great pagoda, with the sunshine glinting on its gilded roof, wet from the recent rain. I recall also the Burmese shopkeepers, whose generosity was once again much in evidence, although on this occasion the Japanese guards seemed much more determined to prevent us from accepting the goods which were offered. Pickings were therefore comparatively poor.

From the dockside at Moulmein, we were marched to the town jail, where we spent the night in a huge communal cell furnished with rows of solid wooden beds which were secured to the floor. At the head of each bed was a rectangular block of wood with a semi-circular depression in the top. These I presume were intended as head rests, but they looked to me so remarkably uncomfortable that I quickly discarded any thought of using them as such. Outside the cell was a compound to which we had free access, and in an adjoining compound I saw Burmese prisoners, chained at the ankles. They were being given their evening meal, crouched on their haunches in cringing groups of half a dozen - a wretched band whose plight seemed worse than ours.

The next morning we were transported by goods train from Moulmein to Thanbyuzayat, a much smaller place some thirty miles to the south. Here we were put in a large prison camp which we quickly discovered was the base camp for the construction of a railway between Burma and Thailand. From Thanbyuzayat, prisoners were being drafted to various points along the proposed route of the new railway, to carry out the necessary spade work and lay the track. This prospect did not cause great concern, but it no doubt would have done if we had known that some years earlier, following a survey, the proposed route had been rejected because of the difficulty of the terrain and the risk of cholera, which was endemic in the area.

The accommodation at Thanbyuzayat was similar to that at Mergui - long narrow huts of bamboo and atap. I observed, however, that inside many of the huts, pasted on the bamboo uprights, were notices in bright red letters which read "WORK CHEERFULLY". These caused much wry and obscene comment.

Organisation within the camp was very efficient, in fact rather too efficient from the point of view of the prisoners, who found themselves all too quickly on their way up country. My group - the Padang party - was no exception. Within three days of arriving, we were despatched to a camp eighteen kilometres along the route of the proposed railway, but before we left we were paraded and addressed in Japanese by the camp commandant, Colonel Nagotomo. He stood on a table to deliver his speech and beside him, also on the table top, there was a Eurasian Dutch prisoner who translated the speech into English, sentence by sentence. The commandant referred to us as "arrogant and insolent imperialists", "skeletons of a rabble army", etc. He warned would-be escapees of the "perils of the limitless jungle to the east, the boundless ocean to the west, and the ever watchful presence of the Nippon Army to the north and south", and threatened that anyone foolish enough to make the attempt would "face the extreme penalty". Having thus thoroughly insulted and threatened us, he ended by enjoining all of us to "work cheerfully". This final remark was no doubt regarded by the vain commandant as an impressive climax worthy of wide publicity; hence the notices in the huts.

By the time the Padang group left Thanbyuzayat it had become generally known as the British Battalion. This was because it happened to be the only UK force employed at the Burma end of the Railway, the majority of UK prisoners having been taken at Singapore and set to work at the Thailand end of the line. At the Burma end most of the prisoners were Australian and Dutch, but there was a small contingent of Americans captured in Java, plus the British Battalion.

The British Battalion at Thanbyuzayat numbered four hundred and eighty three, including twenty officers, all Army men, headed by Captain D P Apthorp of the Royal Norfolk Regiment. Seventeen of our number had died at either Mergui or Tavoy, and when we moved to the

18km camp we left behind about half a dozen more who were too sick to travel.

Chapter Five - Start of the Burma Railway

We set off for the 18km camp on foot. It was a hot day and the road, which was no more than a cart track through the bush, was dry and dusty. Fortunately, lorries were provided for the transport of our baggage and these, after delivering the baggage, made several journeys to and from the marching column, picking up prisoners. Many of us, therefore, including myself, did not have to march the full eighteen kilometres.

As we neared the new camp our lorry halted briefly alongside a small group of Australian prisoners who were working with picks and shovels. Addressing the Australian nearest the truck, a Cockney member of our party yelled out

"Watcha, me ol' Dig!"

The Australian slowly straightened his back and leaned on his pick. Then, looking up at us in the lorry, he pushed back his battered bush hat and said in sepulchral tones with great emphasis

"You'll be fack'n sorry mite."

Before anyone had time to frame a suitable answer to this sour prediction, the lorry moved on, but the feelings of all of us were well summed up by our Cockney friend who commented

"Christ, 'e's got the 'ump."

On reaching the new camp, the lorry halted at what was clearly the Japanese guard house. It was a wooden structure with a veranda at its front and, underneath the veranda, a wooden bench. It put me in mind of a summer house, except that on the bench sat three or four Japanese guards with rifles vertical between their knees. One of them came over to the lorry, walked slowly round it and, after a brief word with the driver, motioned us in. The lorry bumped forward and came to rest in a cloud of dust on a bare patch of earth which appeared to be a parade ground. Here we dismounted, sorted out our individual baggage from the heap which had been piled at the edge of the square, and sat down to await the arrival of the rest of the party.

It was hot and uncomfortable sitting in the glare of the midday sun on the bare earth of the parade ground, and the bleakness of the camp environment did nothing to raise one's spirits. On one side of the square stood the prisoners' accommodation in the shape of the customary bamboo and atap huts, long narrow and parallel to one another, and on the opposite side of the square there was a smaller group of huts, the superior wooden construction of which immediately proclaimed them as quarters for the guards. Outside the camp the land was flat and scrubby except in the distance, where hills were visible.

When the whole of the British Battalion finally arrived, after an hour or so, there was a roll call and food and drink were issued. The food was boiled rice and the drink was boiled water. These rations were brought to us by Australian prisoners who told us that their contingent, which had been working at the camp for some weeks, was five hundred strong and headed by a Colonel Anderson, VC.

When the meal was finished we were divided into what the Japanese call "kumis", and a British officer was put in charge of each. A"kumi", as far as I recall, consisted of about fifty men. We were then led off by Kumis and allocated accommodation in the bamboo huts. These were found to be similar to previous bamboo and atap structures which we had encountered - open along one of the longer sides and with a sleeping platform the full length of the building. The platform, however, was double width, thus providing twice as many bed spaces as the narrower version. Officers had the same accommodation as the men, but grouped themselves together at the end of one of the huts.

In a wooded depression along one side of the camp there was a stream. It was too shallow for swimming but its water was wonderfully cool and during the afternoon we enjoyed a long and refreshing bathe in it, scooping the water happily over ourselves and each other with a remarkable assortment of mess tins, mugs and metal cans.

Towards sundown, shortly after the Australian prisoners who had been working on the line returned to the camp, a bugle was sounded to indicate that the evening meal was ready. It was the Japanese Army call to the cookhouse, but it was so like the British "Come to the cookhouse door, boys," that I felt it must have been copied. The two scores are as follows:

British

repeat

Japanese

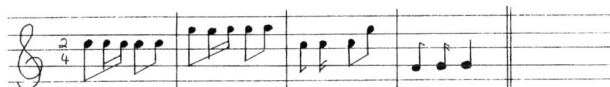

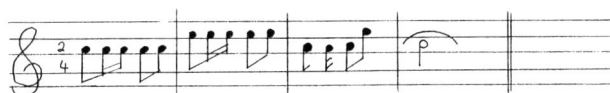

The meal was served in four gallon petrol tins with wire carrying handles, the rice separate from the stew, each kumi sending representatives to fetch the rations from the cookhouse. The individual portions were small, about half a pint of rice and half a pint of stew, but the stew had a slightly meaty flavour and indeed one or two individuals did locate actual pieces of meat. My initial impression of food at this camp was therefore that the quality was probably just adequate, but the quantity insufficient. A few of my kumi on that first evening managed to obtain "leggies", but I was unfortunately too far behind in the original queue to have any chance of a second helping. Second helpings in the Australian lines, incidentally, were referred to as "back ups", and among American prisoners, whom we were to meet further down the line, the expression was "seconds".

After the meal, a role call (or "tenko". as the Japanese called it) was held on the parade ground. Orders on the parade ground were given in Japanese -"kiotski", or more often the abbreviated form "ski", meaning "attention," and "Yasume"(or "sme" in the shorter form) meaning "stand easy". We also had to number off in Japanese, a skill which took the British Battalion a day or two to acquire. The British are notoriously lazy in the field of languages and the British Battalion on the Railway was no exception. So far as Japanese was concerned, apart from parade ground language, which was forced upon us, we picked up only the most essential words, such as "beeokee"(sick), "benjo"(latrine), "mishi-mishi"(rice), "mizu"(water) and "arigato"(thank you). Japanese knowledge of English was also limited, especially among the lower ranks. Communication on the whole was consequently poor, and misunderstandings were frequent. There were, however, interpreters at some of the camps, and for a period at the 18km camp our interpreter was a certain Captain Drower who had lived and worked in Japan and therefore spoke the language fluently. Drower was the sort of character George Sanders would have played. He was tall and handsome and he exuded a confident superiority from beneath the high domed topee which he invariably wore. There were constant arguments between Drower and the Japanese camp commandant, who no doubt regarded Drower as the archetypal British Imperialist. During these arguments the commandant would shout and bawl at Drower and slap his face, but Drower would remain completely unruffled, firmly arguing his case in faultless Japanese. It was an explosive relationship which I often thought might well eventually lead to bloodshed. Perhaps, therefore, it was as well that Drower, after spending only a few weeks at the 18km camp, was posted elsewhere. I never saw him again but I understand that he ended the war in what was known as a "dog kennel". This was a punishment device consisting of a hole in the ground with a wooden covering above. The hole was too small to allow a man to stand upright or lie at full length. In it the victim was imprisoned, often for long periods, fed only on rice and water and forced to urinate and defecate within its confines. In one of these dog kennels, at Kanburi camp in Thailand, the redoubtable Drower was discovered when the Japanese surrendered. He was covered in sores and ill with malaria, but he reportedly survived.

We began working on the Railway the day after our arrival at the 18km camp. Breakfast consisted of a mug of rice porridge(or "pap", as we more often called it) which was served at dawn. This was about 6am local time but the Japanese had advanced the clocks by about two hours, presumably to coincide with Tokyo time. Whether they did this in all the territories which they over-ran I am not sure but the effect in Burma was to put back the sunrise for the duration of the war.

Tenko followed breakfast and those who were fit were then marched off by kumis to the work site, each kumi accompanied by its British officer, whose function was to supervise the labour.

At the work site most of us were engaged on levelling the track site, either by digging on either side and carrying the soil to form an embankment in the centre, or digging a cutting and piling the soil on either side. We worked in gangs of six, which we formed ourselves, and each gang was supplied with a pick, a shovel and two stretchers, made from bamboo and rice sacking, for carrying the soil. Each man had to shift a cubic metre of earth per day, and at the beginning of each day the six cubic metres appropriate to each gang was measured off and pegged out by engineers of the Japanese army. In the middle of the day we had a break of about an hour, when we were served with rice and vegetable soup, brought from the camp, and we were given two shorter breaks at mid-morning and mid-afternoon.

When a gang finished its measured task, it was allowed to return immediately to the camp. Most of the gangs quickly discovered that, even by working as fast as possible, they were not able to finish appreciably early. They therefore ceased to make the effort. However, two or three gangs regularly achieved early finishes. These were the tough boys - birds of a feather who naturally banded together, and it was with obvious pride that they frequently returned early to the camp, sometimes as early as mid-afternoon. This went on for a week or two, until the Japanese decided that if one or two gangs could complete their work so quickly, the other gangs could do likewise, and they increased the daily task to 1.2 cubic metres per man. This was hard on the weaker gangs, but it at least made the tough boys realise the danger of giving more than they had to, and no-one thereafter made any attempt to finish before time.

Work on the line was undoubtedly hard, especially for people such as myself, who had no experience of navvying. Blistered hands, aching limbs and remorseless sun. But I quickly got used to the life. Blisters gave way to useful calluses, limbs became accustomed to regular exercise and I learned to disregard the sweat which poured constantly from my body. I found that there were skills in the use of picks and shovels, and learned them rapidly. The golden rule with the pick is to wield it steadily rather than at constantly maximum force. I also observed that, when working at a vertical soil face, it is preferable to pick horizontally at low level first. The top lip of the face, thus undermined, then falls of its own accord. Shovelling is also an art. The stretcher must be as close as possible to the soil heap and the shovel must be pushed in to the soil at ground level, pressing the knee against the end of the handle to push it the last few inches. The loaded shovel must then be slightly withdrawn before being vertically lifted - but no higher than is necessary - and emptied onto the stretcher.

For working on the Railway, the Japanese provided us with gee strings and most of us, while at work, wore nothing else. There were a few hats of various sorts, and one or two people wore boots, but in most cases the gee string was the sole article of dress. I still have mine. It is a piece of black cloth twenty inches by nine, fitted with a tape to tie round the waist. It barely covers the pertinent parts and would no doubt be considered obscene in mixed company, but in our all male society it was adequate, and quite a sensible garment for hard work in tropical heat. Wearing a gee string for work also preserved one's other clothes which, in the case of most of those who had tried to escape across Sumatra, were pitifully few and remarkably precious.

On returning to camp after a day's work on the Railway, as well as being tired and dirty, we were ravenously hungry. The evening meal, which followed a welcome bathe in the stream, was therefore the high spot of the day. The meal was never sufficient, but the stew was thicker than at midday and it contained some meat. This improved the flavour and, I suppose, slightly increased the nourishment. Our meat ration, for about a thousand prisoners, was one bullock a day. The bullocks, however, having been driven on the hoof from the base camp, were appallingly thin and yielded nothing like the amount of beef which might have been expected from a well fed animal. Never have I seen such wretched bullocks as on the Burma Railway. They were Indian type cattle with the characteristic hump on the shoulder which, combined with ribs which seemed about to burst from the flesh, produced a miserable spectacle.

The evening meal was followed by tenko and, shortly after that, down came the darkness. Lights were not provided, but prisoners gathered in groups outside their huts and lit fires which provided a modicum of illumination. The fires were also a source of cheerfulness, a forum for gossip and a means of cooking anything that might be available. Most people had nothing to cook, especially in the early days at the 18km camp, before the first pay arrived, but one or two groups managed to produce ersatz coffee. This was made from uncooked rice, which was ground by rolling it with a bottle, burned in a tin on the fire, and then boiled in water. It tasted nothing like coffee but there was psychological satisfaction in producing a drink which was not simply boiled water. I also recall making ersatz liver from bullock's blood. We boiled the blood until it was solid and then ate it in slices, but the taste was so awful that the recipe went quickly out of favour. I don't know whether solidified blood has any nutritional value, but I am inclined to think not, judging form the large lumps of it which used to pass through me completely undigested.

On the Railway, the Japanese extended the week to ten days. We worked for nine days and rested on the tenth. On the rest day we washed our clothes, mended them if materials were available, cobbled our footwear, had haircuts, shaved, de-loused, and were supplied with a "doover" with our evening meal. Where the expression "doover" came from I do not know. I have never heard it since. It was a kind of rissole, consisting largely of rice, but containing also a dash of chopped vegetables and meat, was spherical, fried and greatly appreciated.

All prisoners on the Railway were constantly plagued by body lice. These are grey torpedo shaped creatures about a quarter of an inch in length, which infest the seams of one's clothing, lay white pinhead sized eggs and cause irritation by biting. On working days we dealt with them by searching them out and cracking them between our thumbnails.

99

This procedure reduced the discomfort but never eliminated it. On rest days, therefore, we resorted to boiling. For this purposes we were supplied with a large oil drum which we filled with water and heated over a fire. Into it went shorts, shirts, blankets, etc, and, at least for a day or two afterwards, we were lice free.

Not many prisoners had the implements necessary for hair cutting and shaving. Those who did were therefore able to charge for their services and, on rest days particularly, they did good business. Most customers demanded the shortest possible hair style, with clippers applied to the whole of the head. This minimised the number of haircuts necessary and, incidentally, reduced the risk of head lice, cases of which were consequently very few. Shaving was less in demand, many prisoners preferring to grow beards. These apparently did not attract lice.

On the Railway we also encountered crab lice. These insidious little creatures, which look like a crab and are about the size of a small pin prick, entrench themselves and multiply in the hair and follicles of the genital area, where they are likely to remain unnoticed until they become a large and well established colony, biting, breeding and perambulating to the great irritation of the host. I had heard of "crabs" but I had never seen one. When my person was invaded I was therefore particularly slow to recognise the pest and, when I did, committed the classical error of assuming that soap and water would dispose of the problem. Nothing could be further from the truth. Soap is manna to "crabs"; they thrive on it. The problem consequently worsened and I was eventually driven to seek(discreetly) the advice of a New Zealand acquaintance named McLachlan who was an able seaman in the Royal navy and slept next to me. He told me that "crabs" were widespread and marvelled that I was not aware of this. He further informed me that he had had a "dose" himself and that an ointment supplied by the MO had quickly cured the affliction. Thus reassured, especially as to the widespread incidence of the problem(I had felt something of a leper), I went off to see the MO. He registered no surprise, which seemed to confirm that he had had plenty of previous cases, gave me a supply of the vital unguent and told me to shave the affected parts before applying it. I carried out his instructions and, to my great relief, was rapidly made whole.

FROM.
NAME _S. W. SADDINGTON._

NATIONALITY _ENGLISH._

RANK _LEADING AIRCRAFTMAN._

CAMP War Prisoners Camp,
Moulmein, BURMA.

To _T. H. SADDINGTON,_
240, STONEY LANE,
YARDLEY,
BIRMINGHAM,
ENGLAND.

No. 5
Section
Censored

27th January
1943

(name)

Prisoner of War
Mail

IMPERIAL JAPANESE ARMY.

Thanksgiving
27/1/43

I am interned at The War Prisoners Camp at
Moulmein in Burma.

My health is (~~good,~~ usual, ~~poor~~)
~~I have not had any illness.~~
~~I (am) (have been) in hospital.~~
I am (not) working ~~(for pay at~~ ———————— ~~per day).~~
~~My salary is ———— per month.~~

I am with friends _____

AM IN GOOD SPIRITS. KEEP SMILING. AM
THINKING OF YOU ALWAYS. LOVE TO ALL.
From _Stan._

SERVICE DES PRISONERS DE CUERRE .

俘虜郵便

FROM P. O. W. No. 3370
NAME SADDINGTON·S·W.
NATIONALITY BRITISH
RANK LAC .

Camp: War Prisoners Camp,
Moulmein, BURMA.

To

T.H. SADDINGTON
2H0 STONEY LANE
YARDLEY
BIRMINGHAM
ENGLAND

PASSED

P.W. 3541

3|5|43
18 Kill

IMPERIAL JAPANESE ARMY·
I am still in a P. O. W. Camp near Moulmein, Burma,
There are 20,000 Prisoners, being Australian, Dutch, English,
and American. There are several camps of 2/3000 prisoners who
work at settled labour daily.
We are quartered in very plain huts. The climate is good. Our
life is now easier with regard to food, medicine and clothes. The
Japanese Commander sincerely endeavours to treat prisoners kindly.
Officers' salary is based on salary of Japanese Officers of
the same rank and every prisoner who performs labour or duty
is given daily wages from 25 cents (minimum) to 45 cents,
according to rank and work.
Canteens are established where we can buy some extra
foods and smokes. By courtesy of the Japanese Commander we
conduct concerts in the camps, and a limited number go to a
picture show about once per month.
ALL THE BEST KEEP SMILING
ALL MY LOVE. STAN.

SERVICE DES PRISONNIERS DE GUERRE,

From P. O. W. No. *3370.*

Name *SADDINGTON. S. W.*

Nationality *ENGLISH.*

Rank *LEADING AIRCRAFTMAN.*

Camp : No. 3 Branch Thai War Prisoners
Camp. NIKE, THAILAND.

俘虜郵便

昭和19年2月1日
第三分所検閲済
泰俘虜収容所

To *T.H. SADDINGTON,*
240, STONEY LANE,
YARDLEY,
BIRMINGHAM,
ENGLAND.

PASSED
P.W. 3894

IMPERIAL JAPANESE ARMY.

Our present place, quarters, and work is unchanged since last card sent to you. The rains have finished, it is now beautiful weather. I am working healthily ( ). We receive newspapers printed in English which reveal world events.

We have joyfully received a present of some milk, tea, margarine, sugar and cigarettes from the Japanese Authorities.

We are very anxious to hear from home, but some prisoners have received letters or cables.

Everyone is hopeful of a speedy end to the war and with faith in the future we look forward to a happy reunion soon.

With best wishes for a cheerful Christmas.

DON'T WORRY. ALL IS WELL. HOPE TO BE
WITH YOU AGAIN SOON. LOVE TO ALL.

From *STANLEY*

SERVICE DES PRISONNIERS DE GUERRE

NUMBER 3370

Name SADDINGTON. S. W.

Nationality BRITISH

Rank LEADING AIRCRAFTMAN

Camp...... No: 3 P. O. W. Camp,
Thailand.

To:-

T. H. SADDINGTON,
240 STONEY LANE,
YARDLEY,
BIRMINGHAM,
ENGLAND

PASSED

P.W 3305

KANBURI ?

IMPERIAL JAPANESE ARMY

Date 19-5-44

Your mails (and) are received with thanks.

My health is (good, usual, poor).

~~I am ill in hospital.~~

I am working for pay (~~I am paid monthly salary~~).

~~I am not working.~~

My best regards to MOTHER, FATHER, SISTER, JOAN, UNCLE FRED AND KENNETH.

Yours ever,

STANLEY

At the non-commissioned levels, pay on the Railway, although graduated according to rank, was ludicrously low. As an LAC in the RAF I was bracketed with army privates and, at the 18km camp, received ten cents a day - provided I worked. If I was sick and could not work, I received nothing. Thus, allowing for three unpaid rest days, the most I could earn in a thirty day month was 2 Rupees 70 Cents, which is slightly over four shillings in old British money, or twenty pence in the modern currency. Commissioned officers fared rather better. Their pay rates were the same as for the equivalent rank in the Japanese army, and the "no work, no pay" rule did not apply. Indeed, except for a few isolated instances, commissioned officers were not required to work on the Railway. They did, however, suffer some severe deductions from the pay to which they were nominally entitled. Half of it was totally withheld. Part of this, the Japanese said was for deposit in a Tokyo bank and the rest of it was to cover board and lodging. Of the remainder, the officers devoted half to a fund for the care of the sick(both officers and men) and the rest they shared equally irrespective of rank. This system, I understand, provided the officers with a monthly income of about 20 Rupees each at the 18km camp.

Although most of us worked on the Railway, a few - perhaps twenty or thirty - had jobs within the camp. These were the orderly room staff, medical orderlies, canteen workers, cooks and kitchen workers and sanitary men whose main job was latrine digging. They were paid for this work and their jobs were much envied by the rest of us. This was partly because camp jobs were less toilsome than working on the line, and partly because it was believed that perquisites were available to at least some of the camp workers. Cooks and canteen workers were particularly suspected of misappropriation and their jobs were consequently coveted above all others. However, there was one canteen worker of my acquaintance who, despite the cloud of suspicion which hung over all of his kind, deserves the highest praise. This was Leslie Bullock, a sergeant in the RAF. I did not discover until the end of the war that his canteen job had been the cover for the valuable and dangerous work of operating a clandestine radio receiver. The receiver was concealed beneath the false bottom of a four gallon petrol can otherwise used for the storage of peanuts. Regular news bulletins were thus received, and conveyed to a restricted circle. How far the circle extended I do not know, but it was small and tight judging from the fantastic character of the rumours which served as news at my level.

In the canteen at the 18km camp prices of goods varied, but the following are typical:

Eggs	5 cents each
Bananas	2 cents each
Tomatoes	3 cents each
Limes	1 cent each
Brown Sugar	20 cents a mug-full
Peanuts	20 cents a mug-full
Condensed Milk	3 Rupees a tin
Small Cheroots	1 cent each
Cigarette Paper(Rizla)	15 cents a packet

Not all these items were constantly available. Different items tended to appear at different times and, on occasions the canteen ran out of stock completely - an event which gave those of us at the bottom of the payscale the wry satisfaction of being hardly affected.

My purchases at the canteen were generally limited to eggs, bananas and either cheroots or tobacco. I ought to have cut out the cheroots and tobacco in favour of the food items, but smoking was a great comfort and a cheroot certainly provided enjoyment for much longer than a banana. Not that anyone at my level smoked whole cheroots. We shredded them with a knife or razor blade and rolled them into cigarettes. From a single cheroot it was possible to make a good half dozen cigarettes, or more if one rolled thin. Cigarette papers I never bought. They were far too expensive and, incidentally, seldom available. I used instead any kind of paper which came to hand. For some months I used the pages of a guide to Singapore. The paper from this source was glossy and rather thick, but I learned the art of splitting it with a razor blade. This needed care and patience and results were patchy, but such thinner paper as was thus produced was well worth the effort, since it was easier to roll and less acrid in the smoking. Newspaper, which was quite scarce, also served as cigarette paper, so did bibles. The latter had a high sale value, especially if sold page by page, and were consequently sacrificed by non-smokers as well as smokers. Bible pages, being thin, were excellent from the point of view of easy rolling, but their smoking quality was not of the best because of the density of the type which adversely affected the taste. All cigarettes made from makeshift paper had disadvantages. Firstly, there was the inferior flavour; secondly, they were liable to unroll because there was no gum on the paper; thirdly, they needed constant re-lighting(which was inconvenient in our matchless society); fourthly, if you drew on them too strongly, they were likely to burst into flame. With all these problems, plus the crudely strong flavour of the primitively cured cheroots and tobacco, it is surprising the smoking habit persisted so widely, but it did - much to the detriment of one's teeth. By the end of the war the deposit on my teeth was so heavy that the notches between them were entirely filled. It took a WAAF dental assistant some hours to remove this encrustation and, when she had finished, my mouth felt unnaturally large.

I brought back to England some of the tobacco which I had been smoking on the Railway and persuaded my father to try it in his pipe. After a few puffs he pronounced it "poison" and would have no more of it. I did not, however, waste the remainder. When summer came, I soaked it in a bucket of water and used the resulting liquor to spray the blackfly on his runner beans. It was very effective.

Our pay on the Railway was in notes designed and printed by the Japanese, and as soon as this new currency appeared the British rupee became valueless. I recall this particularly because, with my last British rupee, I tried to buy some cheroots from a Burmese trader and was rudely rebuffed.

"No good," he said, roughly thrusting the note back into my hand, "King George finish." Confidence in the Japanese money, however, was short-lived. Prices of all goods quickly began to rise and continued to do so throughout the war. The pay of prisoners of all ranks also rose, but not to the same extent as prices. As far as I can remember, my final wage level was 40 cents a day, and the price of a cheroot by then was about 20 cents - unless one could produce a British rupee or some other form of British currency, or an American dollar, in which case(which was rare) a more reasonable bargain could be struck.

Life generally at the 18km camp was squalid and drab, but one day a dramatic event occurred which considerably brightened our existence. This was the escape of Private Pagani of the 18th Division Reconnaissance Corps(the 18th Division was a body of some eighteen thousand men fruitlessly sent to Singapore a week or so before capitulation). Pagani's decision to escape was the result of an argument he had with the camp medical officer, who was an Australian. He reported sick, claiming that he had malaria, but the MO, after examining him, declared him fit and instructed him to join the working party on the line. The view of our medical officers was that all prisoners who were fit should work. This was to safeguard the genuinely sick whom the Japanese would (and did, on occasion) force out to work when the specified quota of workers was not achieved. Pagani apparently argued strongly against this policy and threatened to abscond rather than work for the Japanese. I doubt if the MO took the threat seriously, but Pagani, it turned out, meant what he had said. I saw him leave the camp, ostensibly to join the workforce, but I never saw him again. It was nine or ten o'clock in the morning when he walked out. He was wearing shorts, socks and boots, and he carried a haversack over his shoulder. he was conspicuously European in appearance - short and thick set, fair skinned and red haired. He had a heavy beard and, emblazoned across the full width of his chest, a huge tattoo depicting a chariot and horses. His absence was discovered at the evening tenko, and the reaction of the Japanese was quite comical. They selected about a score of prisoners and told them to search the scrub around the camp shouting to Pagani that provided he returned to camp he would not be shot. Off went the searchers into the bush, while the rest of us waited on the parade ground in the gathering dusk. For some minutes all was silence. Then up went the first cry:

"Come back Pagani and they won't shoot you."

This caused some tittering, which increased when the same entreaty was heard being shouted from the opposite side of the camp. After that, at short intervals, the message to the escapee could be heard being bellowed from all angles, but at a constantly lessening volume as the search area widened. But to no avail. There was no response from Pagani who, having departed some ten hours previously, I would think was well out of earshot. The pantomime nevertheless continued until it was quite dark. The searchers were then recalled, counted and the parade was dismissed. From information received since the war, I understand that Pagani, on leaving the camp in Burma, headed for Indo China. Here he joined a group of Allied Servicemen who had never been captured. They did eventually surrender and were made prisoner, Pagani successfully concealing the fact that he was an escapee.

The British Battalion spent about two months(November and December 1942) at the 18km camp, and during that period six of its personnel died at Thanbyuzayat. It was the practice to transfer the seriously sick to the base camp, and there were consequently no deaths at the up-country camp. Dysentery was the main killer but we also encountered malaria and, for the first time, the deficiency disease, pellagra. The pellagra victim was Ken Jones, an able seaman of the Royal Navy. His main symptom was a large patch of rough red skin across his shoulders and when he reported sick, the MO prescribed an egg a day, to be supplied from the welfare fund. None of us knew anything about deficiency diseases and the reaction of most of us was therefore that Ken was lucky to have contracted what appeared to be a trivial ailment requiring such enjoyable treatment. Little did we realise that later on the deficiency diseases would become more widespread and more severe, and would prove fatal in many cases. Ken, however, recovered splendidly on his egg diet and survived the rest of the war.

For some weeks at the 18km camp, although I was thin and constantly hungry, I kept remarkably well. Then, very suddenly, dysentery struck again and I was transferred to the camp hospital which, in accordance with army practice, was known as the "RAP", an abbreviation for "Regimental Aid Post". In it, however, there was no aid for dysentery cases. We simply lay there, between increasingly frequent journeys to the latrine. In this environment I remained for four or five days. It was then decided to transfer me, with half a dozen fellow sufferers, to the base hospital at Thanbyuzayat. The journey was by lorry and, as expected, it was a rough ride, the surface of the dusty dirt road being hard and heavily rutted. However, I took precautions against accident by wearing my gee string rather than my shorts, and stuffing half the remnants of a hand-towel between my buttocks.

Chapter Six - The Fury of the South West Monsoon

The exterior appearance of the dysentery hut at Thanbyuzayat was the same as all the other huts on the camp - built of bamboo and atap, long and narrow, a gangway down the centre with a raised sleeping platform on either side. Inside, however, lime had been heavily spread both on the sleeping platforms and on the dirt floor of the gangway. I presume that the lime was to counteract infection, but on me it had a most dispiriting effect. It was as if the inmates were regarded as already dead and being prepared for burial. In these grisly surroundings lay perhaps a hundred men, yellow, listless and skeleton thin.

We were visited daily by a Dutch MO and medical orderlies were in regular attendance, but no treatment was available and one simply survived or succumbed. The food was the same as we had been used to up country. Pap for breakfast, rice and stew at midday and in the evening. At Mergui, in the dysentery hospital, there had been a slogan "eat or die", and I had seen many die after ceasing to eat. At Thanbyuzayat, I therefore resolved to eat at least a little at every meal, and this I did, though whether or not it was a factor in my recovery I shall never know. It is surprising how quickly dysentery demolishes the appetite, especially when the diet is unattractive.

I am not certain how long I spent in the dysentery hut at Thanbyuzayat, but I was there on Christmas Day, which was marked by the issue of a superior stew. There was more meat in it than usual and it was liberally laced with brown beans. I thought it quite an improvement on the normal fare, although it proved highly indigestible and caused considerable discomfort the next day, most of which I spent squatting on the latrine. This was a primitive and unsanitary device, outdoors, at the end of the hut. It consisted of a long rectangular pit with a bamboo cover in which was a line of foot square holes at intervals of about a yard. Its foul smelling yellow liquid contents seethed with maggots and above it there was a constant cloud of flies. This type of privy, which was common to all the camps, was no doubt the best that could be devised in the circumstances, but was far from hygienic and no doubt contributed to the spread of diseases such as dysentery.

From the dysentery hut at Thanbyuzayat I progressed to the convalescent ward, where the atmosphere was more cheerful although, next to me, there was an old Australian seriously ill with malaria. He belonged to an army motor transport unit which he had managed to join by under-stating his age. He was gaunt and grizzle haired and frequently delirious. One morning he opened the waistband of his trousers to reveal the worst infestation of lice I ever saw on the Railway. As he undid the waistband the lice tumbled off it in heaps, onto his belly which was bright red from irritation.

During my period in the convalescent ward the Japanese executed an Australian who had tried to escape. I did not witness the event and I did not know the Australian involved but, according to the account which circulated, the man was simple minded and had returned voluntarily to the camp after a day or two of aimless wandering in the bush. In these circumstances it had been hoped that the Japanese would spare his life but, early one morning, they marched him out of the camp to the nearby cemetery and shot him. Such callous behaviour no prisoner of the Japanese can ever forget or forgive.

After a week or two in the convalescent ward I was moved to a third hut, put on light duties about the camp, and given half pay. Next to me, in my new accommodation, was a fellow airman from the 18km camp, Andrew Macdougall, who was recovering from malaria. He and I naturally chummed up and before long we found ourselves discussing means of supplementing our meagre income. We were not, by any means, the first to consider setting up a business. I have already mentioned the barbers who charged for haircutting and shaving. At Thanbyuzayat there were sellers of coffee(by the cup), sambal(which was a fried concoction of peanuts and chillies), "doovers" of varying kinds and quality, and cigarette paper. You could also get metal cans repaired and, if you had a watch or jewellery or clothes to sell, there were people who were prepared to go over the wire at night and dispose of them on a commission basis. All of these operations were referred to as "rackets", and in the purely social sense that is what they were. They required enterprise, however, and they provided services for which there seemed no shortage of buyers. They were therefore to some extent justifiable and there was certainly never any outcry against them. One of the best known "businessmen" at Thanbyuzayat was Sapper Adrian, a member of the British Battalion whose speciality was coffee. This he hawked round the camp in four gallon petrol cans. "Hot sweet coffee", he used to shout, "champagne of the Orient; five cents a mug". He did a roaring trade and, far from resenting him, people welcomed both his product and his patter. One day, however, his patter, in my opinion, went beyond the seemly. During the previous night a prisoner had fallen(or jumped) into the camp well and been drowned, and Adrian, capitalising on this unhappy event, added to his usual spiel the cry "Plenty of body in it today". What effect this had on his sales I do not know, but no one in my hearing uttered the slightest objection.

Mac and I decided to bake and sell cakes. Rice, which we could get from the "leggy" queue, would be the main ingredient and we would flavour it with sugar and ground ginger root, both of which were available from the canteen and not too expensive in the modest proportions we intended to use. The mix could be put into Mac's round Dutch mess tin, which was about seven inches in diameter and five inches deep, and the baking could be done in the embers of one of the cookhouse fires when the official cooking for the day had finished. We also decided that, in order to obtain the best price for our product, we would aim at the officer market. We put the plan into operation and on the whole it worked very well. There were occasions when the "leggy" queue failed us but generally we managed to produce a cake a day. Dutch officers were our main customers and we charged them 60 cents a time. The turnover was modest but 60 cents was the equivalent of twelve days pay at half rate and the project was therefore well worth while. It certainly enabled us to buy a few extras, notably eggs, and these, coupled with our improving health and the freedom from hard work, made our lives a good deal more tolerable. Indeed the only serious discomfort I recall at this time was the cold nights. The daylight hours were as hot as ever, but during the hours of darkness the temperature fell dramatically and by dawn one's breath was as steamy as on a winter's day in England. In these conditions, and with so little in the way of clothing, sleep became impossible long before the sun rose. Dawn therefore often found many of us huddled in the cookhouse getting what warmth we could from the fires on which the breakfast pap was being prepared. Sometimes, however, too many of us would congregate in the kitchen and the cooks would turn us all out.

During the cake making period at Thanbyuzayat all prisoners were supplied with a postcard to send home. The cards were headed "Service des Prisonniers de Guerre" which gave the impression that the International Red Cross was involved and that therefore, unlike the scraps of paper on which we had hopefully written at Mergui, they would safely reach their destination. Apart from a small space for a personal message, the card consisted of a list of printed sentences most of which contained a choice of words which one selected by deletion of those which were inappropriate. This was not an easy task. One of the sentences read "I am/have been in hospital". I thought it best not to worry my family by saying either that I was, or had been, in hospital, so I struck out the whole of this phrase but, in order to avoid giving the impression that I was in robust health, I also deleted another phrase which read "I have not had any illness". Thus I tried to convey a not-too-alarming picture, without straying too far from the truth. I was not entirely satisfied with the result, but it was the best I could do and I took comfort in the fact that, if the card arrived(which it did), it would at least indicate that I was alive.

Unfortunately, the time came all too quickly when I was judged fit enough to return to work on the Railway. I was naturally glad to be rid of the dysentery, but I was reluctant to leave the comparative ease of the base camp and, more especially, the lucrative little cake business. During my absence the British Battalion had been moved to the 35km camp and I rejoined it there about the middle of February 1943. I had been at the base camp about two months.

The conditions and the routine at the 35km camp were much the same as the 18 km camp, but the daily task had been increased to 1.5 cubic metres per man. This was hard going and meant that, except on the rest day, which continued to be observed, we seldom saw the camp in daylight. Rations, as usual, were inadequate in both quantity and quality and I was constantly hungry, especially at the end of the day when I could have eaten an ox.

Shortly after starting work at the new camp, my only pair of shoes gave up the ghost. For some months sole and upper had been kept together only by a binding of iron wire. This had kept breaking; the soles had flapped and been bent too frequently underneath the foot, causing them eventually to fracture and break off. In this condition the shoes provided hardly any protection and I therefore discarded them. A good many of my fellows had been working barefoot for a long time, so my case was no exception, but I was sorry, nevertheless, to have to abandon a pair of shoes which, in ordinary circumstances, could so easily have been repaired. I replaced the shoes with a pair of flip-flops. These I made from two flat pieces of wood which I roughly fashioned to the shape of the sole. They were kept in place on the foot, somewhat precariously, with a strip of cloth across the instep. They were unsuitable for work on the line but served to keep my feet off the ground when I was in camp.

My next problem was scabies. It started with an itch between the fingers. Then tiny scabs appeared and broke into sores which spread across the hands. I obtained from the MO an ointment made from crushed sulphur tablets mixed with stolen motor grease, but not soon enough to prevent the infection from spreading to the penis, which proved a delicate area to treat, especially as the sulphur was none too finely ground. In the tropical heat, the ointment had a vile stench which contaminated everything I touched, not least my gee string and blanket, the stink of which grew abominable. What was only a minor ailment thus proved remarkably unpleasant and I was greatly relieved when it finally subsided, even though I then had to return to work on the Railway.

At about this time, news was received of the execution at Thanbyuzayat of an Australian army sergeant named Bell. Bell, with two other Australians, had escaped from one of the up-country camps and reached

115

a point well north of Moulmein before being spotted by the Japanese while trying to cross an open paddy field in daylight. The trio had been armed with revolvers and had fought it out with the Japanese, but in the unequal struggle both of Bell's companions had been killed and Bell himself had been wounded before being retaken. Whether or not all of these details are accurate I have no means of knowing, but I have no doubt that the three Australians did make an unusually brave bid for freedom and, in so doing, earned widespread admiration.

News also reached us at the 35 km camp that Second Lieutenant Brockman, a New Zealander belonging to the British Battalion, had died from dysentery at Thanbyuzayat. His was the first death among our officers.

Towards the end of March, much to our surprise, a small group of American prisoners arrived at the 35 km camp. Some of them belonged to the 131st Field Artillery; others were survivors of the cruiser Houston which had been sunk in the Sunda Strait. Most of them hailed from the southern states of the USA and all had been captured in Java. But we hardly had time to make the acquaintance of these new arrivals before both they and the British Battalion were moved back along the line to the 14 km camp. Here, we were engaged on the repair of some earthworks which had subsided. This job we finished in about ten days and for a month or so afterwards the British Battalion was assigned to track laying.

Track laying was a new experience and, on the whole I preferred it to navvying. It had its risks. One had to be careful not to drop a rail or a sleeper on one's foot, especially a bare foot, but the work was less concentrated because it consisted of a number of consecutive operations, each of which was the responsibility of a separate gang. Each gang, at intervals, thus enjoyed some respite.

The rails, etc., were brought to the railhead along the existing track. Each set of rails was supported by a pair of four wheeled bogeys, one at each end, and there were some eight or ten sets of rails in each train. On the top of each set of rails, in corresponding numbers, lay the sleepers, spikes, fishplates and bolts. The trains were pushed by ingeniously designed diesel vehicles which, having pneumatic tyred wheels fitted on the outside of their flanged wheels, were capable of being driven on roads as well as on rails. These diesel vehicles were used on the railway not only in connection with the track laying. They were also used for hauling goods generally on newly laid track which, prior to ballasting, a process which came after the track laying, was unfit for heavy steam engines. The use of diesel vehicles on new track also largely straightened the rails which, on being first laid, looked like a pair of wriggling serpents.

I was in the gang whose job was to unload and lay the sleepers. We carried the sleepers on our shoulders, two men per sleeper and, to protect our shoulders from chafing, the Japanese provided us with flat circular collars made from canvas, much like the mint with the hole, but with the rim split to enable the device to be slipped over the head. I was surprised at such consideration, which seemed to me out of character with the normal Japanese attitude to prisoners.

The sleepers were laid across the intended track of the railway at intervals of a metre, and when sufficient of them were in position a pair of rails was pulled forward from the load by another gang of prisoners. Each rail was guided over a double flanged wheel set in the top of a three foot high tripod. The gang then ran forward with the rail until a man standing at the tripod gave a warning shout and pulled a lever which dropped the wheel from under the rail. The gang had then quickly to let go and step smartly sideways to avoid being struck by the rail as it clanged onto the sleepers. By manhandling and the use of crowbars and sledge hammers, the two new rails and their sleepers were then manoeuvred into their final positions. The new rails were then fishplated to the existing rails and spiked to the sleepers. The required separation of the rails was one metre and this dimension was regularly checked by gauge as the spiking proceeded. On thus completing a rail length of track, by which time further sleepers would have been put in position, the train of rails was pushed forward and the procedure was repeated. As each load of rails was used the bogeys, which had supported them, were lifted from the rails and put at the side of the track. Then, at the end of the day, all the bogeys were put back on the lines and we pushed them back to the camp - except on downhill sections of the track where the bogeys needed no pushing and we rode on them instead.

There were some surprisingly steep gradients at certain points on the Burma Railway and the wood-fired steam engines, when they came into use, sometimes had difficulty in pulling the trains up them. When this happened, and there were prisoners on board, the train would halt and the guards would walk along the line of trucks shouting "Orru may puss, orru may puss": which, being translated meant "All men push". We would then have to dismount and start shoving. It always appeared at first an impossible task to shift these stranded trains, but in fact we never failed to move them. The driver's procedure was to apply full throttle intermittently. This caused loud and rapid snorting by the loco, clouds of smoke and steam and a wild spinning of the engine wheels but gradually, as we pushed, the wheels would begin to grip and the train would stagger forward.

We normally laid a kilometre of track per day but one day we were kept at work for twenty-four hours and laid two kilometres, the second kilometre by the light of flares during the night. We then went back to camp, breakfast and bed, but we were hauled out again at midday to lay a further kilometre, which we did not complete until well after dark. In two days we thus did fifty percent more work than usual and began to fear that the Japanese intended to substitute this new work pattern on a continuous basis. However, our fears proved groundless. The next day we reverted to normal working, much to the relief of all of us.

During the track laying, we stayed at various camps and two of them I recall particularly. The first was the 25 km where the Japanese commandant was a drunken lieutenant named Naito. This lout exhibited his evil temperament on our very first day in the camp. A Burmese woman came to the entrance with a huge basket of eggs and Naito began to converse with her. It appeared that Naito wanted to buy some eggs but was unwilling to pay the price which was asked. At all events he grew more and more angry, eventually overturning the basket and trampling on the contents. The woman fled in panic and Naito then picked up half a dozen or so of the few eggs which had not been broken and took them away with him. In his relations with the prisoners, Naito's behaviour was equally overbearing. He delighted in stopping and haranguing men for no clear reason. On these occasions, the victim had to stand rigidly to attention while Naito, gesticulating wildly with his revolver, poured forth a slurred mixture of incomprehensible Japanese and English. He was also given to making us parade in the middle of the night while our huts were searched on the pretext that we were harbouring Burmese women. Another unnerving nocturnal habit of his was suddenly to thrust his torch through the atap wall of a hut and shine it in the face of the nearest sleeping prisoner. But his childish vanity was most pathetically displayed when he had to go to the base camp at Thanbyuzayat. He travelled in an armchair on an open railway truck and the prisoners, standing to attention at the edge of the track had to salute him as he departed. It was difficult for Naito to return the salute, partly because of his inebriated condition and partly because of the motion of the train, but he accomplished it on both occasions when I was involved in this ridiculous ceremony.

I also recall, at the 25 km camp, a film show which the Japanese put on for our entertainment. The show was given in the open air one evening in a part of the camp where there happened to be a natural amphitheatre. The first film was of a Japanese woman singing to the accompaniment of a piano. She may very well have been highly regarded in her native environment but to our western ears her oriental caterwauling was a painful experience. Then came the feature film which was a propaganda piece extolling the courage of the Japanese airforce in its attack on Pearl Harbour. The effect of this film on me was to underline the innate treachery of the Japanese character.

At the 25 km camp we also had a case of smallpox, and there was some concern that the disease would spread, but it did not, partly perhaps because the patient was strictly isolated but more likely, in my opinion, because of the vaccination which in the British Forces is compulsory on joining. The victim was Able Seaman Thomas and, thanks to the devoted care of a Dutch doctor named Captain Hekking, he recovered.

Thomas told us afterwards that by some sort of deception he had purposely evaded the customary vaccination in the Navy.

The other camp which I particularly associate with my plate laying days was the 45 km. It was one of the worst that I encountered. The huts were dilapidated, the site was contaminated with flies, excrement and the remains of food, and underneath one of the sleeping platforms we found a dead Indian. We buried the Indian and cleaned up the place as well as we could but, when we lay down to sleep, we were attacked by bed bugs. These are brick coloured insects about a quarter of an inch across and shaped rather like plaice. They bite and irritate and, when crushed by the writhings of the sleeper, give off a foul smell. The presence of these pests at first caused nothing more than tossing and turning, but within half an hour we were all outside the huts desperately shaking our bedding and clothes. This procedure had to be continually repeated throughout the night and, as a result, we got very little sleep. What surprised me was the speed with which the infestation was identified. Most of us had no experience of bed bugs, but there were some among us who clearly had. Indeed, one of our number, a Glaswegian, informed us that at home his mother used Keatings Powder to deal with the problem. Unfortunately, no such remedy was available to us. We could therefore only continue to employ the manual control method, which was of very little effect. I was consequently much relieved when, after three or four sleepless nights, we once again moved, this time back to the 18 km camp.

On our arrival at the 18 km camp we were given our second postcard to send home. It was similar to the earlier one but provided no choice of message. I had no objection to "we are quartered in very plain huts", but I felt that statements such as "our life is now easier with regard to food, medicine and clothes", and "the Japanese Commander sincerely endeavours to treat prisoners kindly" were likely to give a very false impression of our circumstances. However, better that my family should be misled on detail rather than receive no word at all. So I sent off my card. And it was duly delivered.

In our absence the 18 km camp had been rebuilt and converted to a transhipment depot where rails, sleepers, rations and goods generally were unloaded from steam trains, stacked and stored, and then reloaded onto diesel trains for conveyance further up the line. We worked twelve hour shifts, one in daylight and one during the night. The best job was ration handling, partly because it was comparatively light work and partly because it was thought to offer opportunities for thieving. The food, however, was well guarded and not easy to "lift". I recall acquiring, during a daylight shift, some tomatoes which were passed to me through the broken floorboards of a box wagon, and a strip of dried fish which I managed to remove from a basket during a night shift, but nothing else of significance. The rail handling was much heavier work. Each rail, I suppose, was about five metres in length and needed a dozen or so men to lift it. Often the individual effort was patchy and a rail would remain rooted to the ground. This would incense the guard, who would run along the line of stooping prisoners bawling at them and kicking their backsides. This procedure rapidly restored our co-ordination.

Our stay at the 18 km camp was brief, no more than two or three weeks. The British Battalion and its transhipment activities were then transferred to the 30 km camp. Here the conditions were much as before, except that we now had to contend with the south-west monsoon. This descended on us with little warning at the beginning of June, bringing continual rain, leaden skies and low temperatures. Working in such weather would have been unpleasant enough even if we had been adequately clad, but in our naked state it was total misery. My working attire at this stage consisted of gee string, straw hat and rice sack, the rice sack, which was about a yard square, draped around my shoulders. Dressed thus, it was agony each morning to have to step out of the shelter of the hut into the chilling deluge, bare feet squelching in the clammy mud. When we returned to our quarters at the end of the day's work we certainly hadn't far to look for washing water. It cascaded endlessly from the roofs of the huts and we had only to stand under the eaves. Thus washed, I would put on my leisure gear consisting of green patched khaki shorts and cotton singlet, my blanket round my shoulders and flip-flops on my feet.

It surprised me that in such conditions we didn't all die of pneumonia, but in fact there was only one case of this illness - Stan Vaisey, and he recovered. Deaths among the British Battalion did, however, increase, and during June and July the toll was nine. One of these deaths, that of Lance Corporal Oldfield, was said to have been caused by cholera. This surprised me because cholera normally strikes on an epidemic scale and Oldfield's was the only case. However, his symptoms, violent diarrhoea and vomiting, were typical and he died very quickly, which is also characteristic of cholera. Two others of the British Battalion were killed at about this time by Allied bombs which were dropped on Thanbyuzayat base camp. This tragic attack by our own aircraft caused in all some fifty casualties among prisoners of various nationalities who were in the camp at the time, and led to the camp being evacuated a few days later. The prisoners were transferred to various other camps along the railway, the 18 km, the 14 km, etc. and most of them, although sick, some of them desperately so, had to make the journey on foot. On the day of the raid on Thanbyuzayat, my friend Macdougall, was still there. He had, however, by then transferred his endeavours from cake making to toffee making and was in process of cooking his new product when the bombers struck. In the confusion of running for shelter, the tin containing the toffee was upset and the whole day's output was lost, but Mac escaped injury in the raid and shortly afterwards joined me at the 30 km camp.

The guards at the 30 km camp were less vigilant than previously, thanks to the weather, which made them more anxious to keep dry than keep watch. I was therefore able to carry out some useful thieving of beans, tomatoes, onions and other valuable foodstuffs. These I passed to my friend McBain who had the job of medical orderly to the working party and for this purpose was provided with a shoulder bag bearing a large red cross. There was no guarantee that this bag would not be searched, but it in fact never was and we used it regularly for taking our pickings back to camp.

The 30 km camp is also memorable for the newspapers which were supplied to us there. One of them was titled "The Greater South East Asia Co-Prosperity Sphere", or something very similar. The title of the other one I cannot remember but both were in English. The war news they contained was unreliable but one could read between the lines to some extent. For instance, in several succeeding issues of one of these papers there were accounts of Allied air attacks on various islands in the Solomon group. All of these attacks were reported as successfully repulsed by "Nippon's gallant air eagles" but we knew at least that there was persistent activity in the area and we surmised that since the Allies were maintaining their attack they were probably not being quite so decisively repelled as the Japanese newspapers made out. Unfortunately, a single copy of one of these newspapers had to suffice for as many as a hundred men, and by the time it reached the end of the line it was in an extremely dilapidated condition. This was not only because of the constant handling but also because nearly everybody through whose hands it passed would tear off a strip or two for rolling cigarettes. The first part to be removed would be the margins, which was not a serious matter. Then the advertisements would go, often with loss of reading matter on the reverse side, and finally people would remove what they considered inessential news items. The last man on the circulation list thus received not so much a newspaper as a ragged bundle of variously shaped scraps of newsprint barely hanging together. Everyone complained about this and at the same time continued to detach his share of paper for cigarettes. There was consequently no improvement, but the problem was slightly alleviated by varying the order of circulation. This ensured at least that everyone occasionally received a newspaper which was relatively intact.

After a month or so of transhipment work at the 30 km camp I was transferred to a working party formed to repair an embankment which the monsoon rains had eroded. The embankment was a mile or so from the camp, in open country without the slightest shelter. We were thus exposed to the deluge from the moment we left camp in the morning until we returned at night. We even had to eat the midday meal, which was brought to us along the railway, standing in the rain. The work consisted of digging and carrying in the same fashion as we had done when constructing the track, except that the soil was now mud. Indeed the whole site was mud and we were up to our ankles in it most of the time. Every day we worked until dark. It was therefore difficult to see our way back to the camp, difficult, that is, to see our way back at any speed, the speed being necessary in order to secure a forward position in the ration queue, and hence a chance of "leggies". One of the consistently more successful among us, in this nightly race back to the camp was Bungey Edwards. He seemed to have the eyes of a cat and was always well up with the leaders. But his luck ran out. He was striding confidently forward as usual one night when he suddenly gave a terrible cry of anguish followed by a string of oaths which rapidly faded away in the distance. It was as if he had been suddenly snatched up and borne aloft by some powerful unseen force. But when we reached the point of his disappearance it became clear that he had fallen down the bank of a ravine at the approach to a bridge. Unlike bridges in more civilised areas, those on the Burma Railway had no guard rails at their ends. The only safe way to approach them in darkness was therefore along the middle of the track. Otherwise, one ran the risk of stepping into the void across which the bridge was built. Bungey, hastening along the side of the track, had forgotten the existence of the bridge and paid the inevitable penalty. Judging from the moans and curses which came to us from the depths, I expected him to be seriously injured but when he was hauled back up to track level it was clear that no bones were broken. He suffered some bruises and grazes, however, which considerably reduced the speed at which he completed his journey back to the camp.

One other noteworthy event occurred at the 30 km camp. This was the issue of some boots. There were not enough to equip everyone who needed them, many of the sizes being too small to fit anybody, but I was one of the lucky ones. The boots were brown leather, lightweight and rather smart. I put mine on in some excitement, laced them with care and proceeded to test walk them up and down the gangway of the hut. Others, similarly fortunate, did likewise, stamping back and forth with exaggerated knee movements in their pleasure at once again feeling leather on their feet. On the following morning when we trooped off to work, it was, as usual, raining heavily. It was therefore comforting to have boots on the feet. But as the day wore on, and the rain continued, the boots began to fail. They became sodden as if made of chamois leather, soaking up the water instead of repelling it, and giving one the impression of being shod in sponges. This was extremely disappointing, but I felt that the new boots, although obviously not waterproof, would still provide the feet with a measure of protection. However, when we returned to camp in the evening and peeled off the boots, there were clear signs of rupture of the material, particularly at the lace holes. We continued to wear the boots for some days but gradually they disintegrated completely. Uppers tore, soles came away and it became impossible to secure them to the feet. Wire binding was resorted to by some, but all to no avail. The boots became useless and we discarded them in disgust.

Chapter Seven - Lowest Ebb

Our next camp was the 60 km, where we arrived about the middle of July. Here the food, work and weather were much as at the previous camp, except that we were more involved with rails than with rations, and opportunities for filching food were consequently fewer. I recall this fact because food, or rather the lack of it, was a constant preoccupation. We had never been adequately fed since being captured, and as the work demanded of us increased, so did our appetites. Food was therefore a permanent obsession. The long "leggy" queues which formed at every meal time were constant evidence of this, so was the eagerness with which the rations of men too sick to eat, were absorbed by their friends. It was natural enough not to waste the rations of a sick man lacking appetite, but I felt that in some instances there was a marked lack of effort in trying to persuade the patient to eat.

Dysentery and malaria continued to plague us, as they had done since Mergui, but tropical ulcers and beri-beri now began to afflict us as well. There had been the occasional ulcer in the past, but they now became much more common. They appeared chiefly on the legs and were the result of abrasions of various kinds, often so small as not to be initially noticeable. The ulcers developed very suddenly, grew rapidly in both depth and diameter, quickly filled with yellow pus and were extremely difficult to heal. The only treatment was to spoon out the pus. This was a painful operation performed at least once a day at the camp RAP, and in the worst cases the patients had to be held down to keep them still enough for the medical orderly to carry out the gouging. No medicaments were available, dressings were limited and bandages almost non-existent. Ulcers were thus a big problem and as time went on and our general health grew steadily worse, the problem increased.

Beri-beri was caused by lack of vitamin B. Early cases were mild, involving generally no more than a watery swelling of the ankles which yielded to rest and a limited water intake. Later on the disease presented in more acute form, causing swollen pendulous jowls, enlarged testicles and a gross thickening of the legs which made walking difficult and painful. It was said that death from beri-beri came when the fluid reached the heart, but whether or not this is true I do not know. Certainly those who succumbed often did so very suddenly. The tragedy of beri-beri on the Railway was that, unlike infectious tropical diseases such as dysentery and malaria, it could so easily have been prevented(and cured) by the provision of a reasonable diet, not a rich or expensive diet, but a diet containing a modicum of common ingredients such as fruit, vegetables, meat or eggs. There is no doubt the Japanese were well aware of this, but in their callous contempt of their captives they made not the slightest effort to provide any of these vital foodstuffs.

The continuing wet weather was an added misery and no doubt adversely affected constitutions already severely weakened by poor diet, lack of clothing and inadequate medical supplies. It would be an exaggeration to say the rain was ceaseless, but there were very few days during the wet season, which lasted from about May to October, when rain did not fall, and there were certainly periods when for days on end the rain was literally ceaseless. Exposure to the rain was bad enough, but we had the additional problem of not being able to dry the few clothes we had. I remember particularly my own regular failure to dry the rice sack which I used as a cape. The only source of heat available was the dying embers of the cookhouse fires, and it was never adequate. I therefore eventually decided to stop making the attempt, although I regularly regretted the decision each morning on donning the damp sack.

Night shifts in the rain were particularly depressing. Before leaving the camp for night work on the sidings we would parade outside the orderly hut to be counted and have our names checked. This task was the responsibility of Sergeant Burgoyne who, wearing boots and waterproof cape, would briskly emerge from the hut with his clipboard, call the roll in a resounding voice, and smartly withdraw to the shelter of his billet for the rest of the night. I tried not to envy Sgt Burgoyne, but as we trudged off into the night I couldn't help feeling how fortunate he was to be so well equipped against weather which he so seldom had to face.

The sidings were half a mile or so from the 60 km camp along a muddy track through scrub, and on moonless nights, owing to night blindness, I found it impossible to see my way. No-one else seemed to suffer from this problem; it was therefore something of an embarrassment. However, an obliging Irishman, whose name I never knew, used to let me hold the tail of his jacket, and by this means I managed to avoid the major obstacles.

On these night marches in the rain there was very little conversation. The main sound was of feet splotching through mud and water. It was a surprise therefore, one night, when Jock Baker, a fellow airman who hailed from Ayr, suddenly announced in a loud voice that he had "the driest pair of boots in the camp". This was clearly not true, it being common knowledge that the sole of at least one of Jock's boots had become largely detached from its upper and flapped noisily in the mud with every step. His statement was therefore vigorously challenged from all sides, but Jock replied "Ah'm dam' certain they're the driest boots in the camp; the buggers are tak'n a drink oot of ivery puddle". This caused a great gust of laughter which obviously puzzled the guard who was marching beside me.

"Nanda," he muttered, reproachfully.

The sidings were a dismal place at night. Bleak lines of trucks, sleepers in dark compact heaps, cold stacks of glistening rails and, over all, the slanting rain, palely illuminated by overhead lights. I detested the place, and the work we had to do there which, more often than not, was the unloading and stacking of rails. For this purpose a crude slipway was constructed by placing two inclined rails against the side of the load. On the ground, from the foot of the inclined rails, further rails were laid, partly to act as horizontal runners, and partly as a base for the first layer of the stack. As the rails clanged down from the load and slithered to a halt on the horizontal runners, a gang on the ground manoeuvred them into close parallel formation with ends flush. When a layer was complete, the two inclined rails were raised at their foot, new runners were laid and the next layer was built. It was tiring monotonous work.

After a month or so at the 60 km camp, a section of the British
Battalion, including myself, was transferred to the 84 km camp.

We made the journey by goods train at night. It was raining and, to
avoid the worst of the weather, instead of climbing onto an open wagon,
two or three of us got into the tender of the engine. Here the cab of the
engine provided a certain amount of shelter and, in order to make the
most of this, we set about clearing the area closest to the cab by
throwing logs from the front to the rear of the tender. The Indian
fireman, thus largely separated from his fuel supply, protested strongly,
so we compromised by throwing onto the footplate a good heap of logs
which we from time to time topped up as the journey proceeded. It was
a slow journey with frequent stops, and when the train was at a
standstill the cab did not provide much shelter, but when the train was
in motion, not only was the rain effectively deflected but we also
experienced a welcome draught of warm air from the footplate.

When we arrived at our destination, to the familiar sound of clanging
rails, it was still dark. We dismounted and were marched to the camp
which stood on a hillside overlooking the sidings. The hut we were
allocated was new but unfinished, half its length having no roof, I
managed to get a place under the roof but some were not so lucky. Next
morning, responding to an early call of nature, I emerged from the hut
and, a short distance form it came across one of our number, Second
Lieutenant Roger Villiers, lying wrapped in a ground sheet in waist
high grass. I thought at first that some dreadful tragedy had befallen him
but as I stood looking down at him he opened an eye and wished me
good morning. I returned the greeting and carried on.

We spent a day or two completing the roof of our hut and were then put
to regular work on the sidings. The day was divided into three eight
hour shifts, and initially I found myself on what became known as the
evening shift. The finishing time of this shift was 1 o'clock in the
morning and it presented me with a recurring difficulty which I
particularly recall. This was the problem of removal of mud from my
feet before getting under the blanket. There was no light in the hut and

the washing process thus had to be carried out in total darkness. My water supply amounted to about a third of a pint which I kept under the sleeping platform in a can which otherwise was used for drinking water. The first objective on returning to the billet was to locate the tin can in the darkness, without knocking it over. This accomplished, the next problem was to wash off the thickly caked mud by feel alone and without running out of water half way through the process. This was difficult, and dawn inspection generally revealed a considerable amount of muck.

From the evening shift I was transferred to the night shift. I was glad to be relieved of the blind foot washing operation, but not so happy having to rise from bed at 1 am to start work. It was Mr Villiers's job to rouse us for the night shift and he did so by walking up and down the central gangway of the hut calling "It's 1 o'clock boys and there's pap in the kitchen". This message was monotonously repeated in a subdued voice calculated to disturb as few as possible of the day shift men, who had the right to continue sleeping. Inevitably however some of the day shift men were disturbed and responded with remarks such as "Belt up!" and "Piss off!". while large numbers of night shift men remained silent and immobile. Mr Villiers thus had a very difficult job. I don't think any of us on the night shift seriously contemplated not getting up. Such action would have been suicide, but it did take a deal of willpower to get out from the blanket at that hour of the morning and face the monsoon rain which was all too evident in the silence of the night, battering down on the palm leafed roof of the hut. We did eventually, and with great reluctance, haul ourselves from our beds, but with much grumbling and swearing. Our low spirits on one occasion, however, were temporarily revived by one of Jock Baker's jokes which, I am sorry to say, was at the expense of Mr Villiers.

"Mr Villiers! Mr Villiers!" said Jock.

"Yes, what is it Baker?" said Mr Villiers, turning towards the sound of the voice.

"Mr Villiers, did you say it was one o'clock, Sir?" asked Jock.

"Yes it is one o'clock,: replied Mr Villiers.

"And did you say there was pap in the kitchen, Sir?" asked Jock.

"Of course there's pap in the kitchen," replied Mr Villiers, somewhat testily.

"Well, here's a gunny sack", said Jock, "top the bugger up."

It was during a nightshift at the 84 km camp that I experienced some violence at the hands of one of the Japanese army engineers who supervised us. We were unloading rails and, as usual, it was raining. There was a lack of enthusiasm on the part of the prisoners and there had been some angry outbursts from the Japs, cries of "speedo", "kurra", "bageero", etc. I don't think I personally committed any offence. I just happened to be the nearest available prisoner for the venting of some wrath. I was at the end of the line of men lifting a rail when suddenly, as I bent over the rail, a fist smashed into my face and I was knocked sprawling on my back. It took me a moment or two to realise what had happened. I then slowly raised myself to a sitting position in the mud and noted that my glasses were gone and my nose was pouring blood. I expected a further attack, but instead the Jap gave me a playful kick on the thigh and barked "You! Yasume!" I got unsteadily to my feet and sat down on a pile of sleepers, wondering at the strange mixture of crude brutality and grudging concern. The Jap stood a pace or two away eyeing me and muttering in a surly fashion. The blood continued to flow, into my mouth and down my chin. I tried to wipe it away, but with muddy hands I didn't have much success. After watching me for a minute or two the Jap came over to me, took hold of my head and pushed it backwards. I thought for a moment he was going to hit me again, but when no blow fell I realised he was trying to stop the blood flow. But the blood kept coming and I remember thinking I couldn't afford to lose much more of it. I found it difficult, in the sitting position, to keep my head bent backwards and I was considering lying flat on my back when the Jap suddenly took from his leather satchel two sheets of paper which he rolled into plugs and stuffed up my nostrils.

"You yasume," he said, "work finish," and strode off. I took this to mean (rightly as it turned out) that I was excused work for the rest of the night, and I was glad enough of the concession, although I would have much preferred to be sent back to the camp where I ould have got some shelter instead of having to sit on a pile of wet sleepers in the pouring rain.

Shortly after the departure of the Jap I remembered my glasses and decided I must try and find them. This proved easier than expected, despite the sea of mud and the limited light. But they were damaged. A lens was missing and the rim of the empty eyepiece was broken. This was a disappointment, but I thought that if I could find the lens I might be able to carry out a repair. So I started to look, probing with a stick and feeling with my hands in the ankle deep mud. I must have spent half an hour prodding about, but to no avail, and eventually I gave up, defeated.

The night passed slowly, the rain persisted and the only comforting thought which crossed my mind was that my nose had apparently stopped bleeding. I kept thinking about the lost lens and when dawn came I decided to make one last attempt to find it. I didn't have much hope, but in fact I spotted it very quickly, and without the slightest effort, standing on its edge in the slush. I wiped the mud off and to my great delight found it completely undamaged. Thus the night shift ended. In terms of physical damage I had escaped comparatively lightly, but I felt humiliated and angry, and I yearned for revenge.

I spent, I suppose, five or six weeks at the 84 km camp, five or six weeks of increasing hardship and misery. It was a period of "speedo" when the Japanese, anxious to complete the Railway, put maximum pressure on the prisoners and increasingly denied them their most basic requirements. The food supply in particular deteriorated sharply. Fresh meat supplies had never been sufficient. They now ceased completely and we instead received dried meat packed in wooden boxes. Most of this our medical officers condemned out of hand. Little of it therefore ever reached the stewpot. Fresh vegetables were also in short supply, in fact the only continuously available fresh vegetable which I can recall was the white radish. Apart from this item our vegetables consisted mainly of dried peas and beans. On this diet, the incidence of beri-beri-rose alarmingly and it wasn't long before I began to notice the typical swelling in my own ankles. This didn't greatly worry me at first because the swelling subsided during the night, but then I reached a stage where the swelling did not disappear at night and became acute during the day. I also developed two ulcers on one of my shins. These grew in size and at the same time the swellings from the beri-beri crept higher up my legs. I did now become concerned and went to see the MO. He had no remedy for the beri-beri but I was given two small squares of lint to cover the ulcers. I fortunately had a bandage of my own which I had kept since the Tavoy days and this I used to keep the lint in place. I was excused work and spent the next few days in camp. I was then sent, with others who were sick, back to the 60 km camp.

Treatment of ulcers at the 60 km camp was much the same as elsewhere on the line, a daily gouging and a fresh dressing, if dressing it could be called, bearing in mind that it consisted only of a clean piece of lint. Each evening, however, I gave the ulcers an extra clean-out myself, with water I heated in my drinking can, and I think this helped, although I had to re-use the soiled dressings which had been on the ulcers all day. At the back of my mind throughout this period was always the fear of gangrene and amputation. These were the ultimate risks with ulcers which would not heal, and in the primitive conditions on the Railway they caused many deaths. My ulcers did eventually heal but it was a slow and painful process. The beri-beri also gradually receded but did not entirely disappear from my ankles until the early part of the following year(1944) when we were taken to Thailand where the food considerably improved.

It was during my second sojourn at the 60 km camp that I received letters from home, about half a dozen of them, all at the same time and all from my father. They had been written a year or so earlier and appeared not to have been censored, nothing in them having been struck out. They were full of detail of Montgomery's victories in the Desert, including the Battle of El Alamein and the joyful ringing of the church bells in England. Those letters were the first and only hard news of the war I ever had whilst I was a prisoner. They were therefore a great boost to my morale and I read and re-read them for many weeks before eventually converting them to valuable cigarette paper. This seemed at the time a sensible enough final use for the letters but I have often since thought that if I had preserved them they would have made interesting reading for my grandchildren. Many other prisoners at the 60 km camp received letters at the same time as I did, but some did not and were plainly disappointed.

My glasses, which had been damaged at the 84 km camp, I never did repair. I thought about the problem many times but there seemed no way of mending the fractured rim and I eventually put them away, resigned to do without them. I then discovered from my friend McBain, who was a medical orderly at the RAP, that there was a small stock of disused spectacles which had belonged to prisoners who had died. He showed me these; there were about half a dozen pairs but, as feared, none of them proved suitable for my eyes. However, one of the pairs had eyepieces which seemed about the same size as mine and I decided to try to replace the lenses in this pair with the lenses from my own glasses. I wasn't at all hopeful but surprisingly I succeeded without much difficulty. Quite a moderate pressure with the thumbs removed the unwanted lenses and also the lens which was still in my own glasses, then in went my own lenses with a very satisfying snap. The success of the operation amazed me and I marvelled at my good luck. It was a great pleasure once again to be able to discern and identify distant objects and I resolved that in future I would take the greatest care of the means of doing so.

I also acquired at the 60 km camp a second blanket. This, like the spectacles, had belonged to a deceased prisoner. It was a poor sort of article, being largely made apparently from cotton rather than wool, and very thin. But I used it, folded double, to put underneath me when asleep. It thus provided some useful insulation which my rice mat alone had never done. I got the second blanket by stating that my existing blanket was worn out. This was true in the sense that the old blanket had certainly become very threadbare. It was, however, still capable of providing a modicum of warmth and of protecting me against mosquitoes. I therefore kept it and continued to use it as a top cover.

Sixteen of the British Battalion died at the 60 km camp and we lost a further twenty at the 55 km, which now served as the hospital base camp for the Burma section of the railway. The facilities at the 55 km were primitive in the extreme, far worse than at Thanbyuzayat. Its task of treating the growing numbers of extremely sick prisoners was therefore exceptionally difficult and its death rate was very high. Miracles were nevertheless wrought there, including some successful amputations with the crudest of equipment. How many of the British Battalion emerged alive from the 55 km I do not know but Alf Hinton, a private in the army, was one of the few, and I recall his name particularly because he recounted to me an unfortunate experience which befell him in the dysentery ward of that frightful place. It was the middle of the night and Alf was suddenly seized by a powerful urge to defecate. The journey to the commode at the end of the hut was perilous enough in daylight; in the pitch blackness of night, with only a sense of feel to guide one, it was doubly hazardous. However, exercising superhuman control, Alf reached his objective without mishap and gratefully, but without a moment to lose, plonked his backside on what he thought was the seat of the commode. Immediately there were frantic cries of "Geroff! Geroff!" But it was too late. The explosion had occurred and all Alf could do was to murmur "Sorry mate; I didn't know you were on it!"

Of the sixteen deaths which occurred at the 60 km, Kelly's in particular remains in my memory. Kelly was a fellow airman and he died, as many others did, worn out by privation and a long series of various illnesses, his last months a continual pattern of recovery and relapse. His body was sewn in the customary rice sack and we carried it to the grave on a bamboo stretcher. The burial service was read, a bugler sounded the last post and our mournful job was over. But that evening, at tenko, the Japanese refused to believe that the reduction of one in our total number was the result of a death. I don't know whether or not it was customary to show the Japanese the body of every prisoner who died, but I think not since, if such had been the established rule, I cannot imagine that it would have been flouted in this isolated instance. However, the Japanese were adamant. They insisted on seeing the body and we had no option but to exhume it. It was as if our captors were determined to humble even our dead.

The Railway was completed in October 1943 and shortly afterwards, over a period of three or four weeks, the majority of the British Battalion were gradually transferred to the 114km camp. Built on a hillside in mountainous country close to the Burma/Thailand border, tightly enclosed by tall jungle trees and frequently enveloped in low damp cloud, this camp had an atmosphere of isolation which chilled the spirit and gave one the feeling of being totally out of reach of all succour, especially at night, when the cloud was at its lowest and condensation dripped mournfully down from the trees. Occasionally at night the drone of high flying aircraft would be heard, but otherwise there was a deep silence. In the daytime, the sounds of camp life and the whooping of monkeys in the surrounding trees, relieved the sense of isolation to some extent, but often the cloud did not lift until gone midday.

At this god-forsaken place, the British Battalion reached its lowest ebb. Here we experienced the worst ever rations and the highest incidence of both sickness and death. Pap(as always) was the staple breakfast; at midday we were given rice with a white radish soup, and in the evening rice with a muddy blue coloured soup made from beans. These two soups we christened "white death" and "blue death" respectively, which I suppose shows that privation had not entirely robbed of us of our sense of humour. Such flippancy, however, did nothing to stem the inexorable rise in the death rate, which reached its peak in December 1943. In that month twenty four of the British Battalion died at the 114km. Considerable gloom was consequently cast over Christmas, especially as we buried two on Christmas Eve and another on Boxing Day. Rations on the festive day also did nothing to rouse the Christmas spirit, the only enhancement to the menu being a teaspoonful of sugar each with the morning pap. It had been rumoured that bananas would be issued, but these did not materialise.

No work of any significance was required of us during the two or three months which we spent at the 114 km. This at least was a blessing, for I believe that if we had had to continue labouring, very few of us would have survived. We were worn out, starving and, in many cases, ill, especially with beri-beri, which hardly anyone escaped. Advanced cases of this illness were pitiful. Distortions of the feet and legs reduced walking to a painful shuffle, and swellings of the face created a bloated mournful look. Our medical officers had no means of treating it beyond advising the victims to drink as little as possible. Many of the victims, however, seemed unnaturally attracted to water. Whether this was because thirst was a feature of the illness, or because the prohibition caused a perverse desire, I do not know, but at all events, when drinking water was available, which was twice a day, at set times, the beri-beri patients were invariably first in the queue.

I have already mentioned that death often struck the beri-beri sufferer very suddenly, and I recall two particular instances of this at the 114 . Both were sailors. The first was Able Seaman Wignall, who came from Nottingham. Wiggy, as he was known, had a chess set, and one particular afternoon I played two or three games with him. He was suffering form beri-beri but I had seen far worse cases. He was cheerful, played sensibly, and betrayed no sign of impending death. The following afternoon there was a burial and when I asked who had died I was told it was Wignall. The second case was Leading Seaman Livermore. We were lying on the sleeping platform in our hut, waiting for the call to evening tenko. We were perhaps two or three yards apart and we were chatting. I put a question which he did not answer and when I repeated it he still made no reply. I thought he had dozed off and, since it was almost time for tenko, I thought I had better wake him, but when I went over to him it was clear that he was dead. He was on his back, head turned slightly sideways, eyes and mouth half open. Such sudden exits from life invariably shock and, although Livermore was not a close friend of mine, his abrupt end obsessed me for some days. The words of the burial service kept crossing my mind "in the midst of life we are in death". Awful words, uncomfortably pertinent.

Ulcers also were a great bane. Starved, exhausted bodies provided the ideal host for this affliction, and grossly inadequate medical facilities ensured maximum difficulty in the treatment of it. Legs swathed in what passed for bandages were everywhere, and were especially evident outside the RAP each morning, where sufferers would queue for the daily gouging. The worst ulcer, however, which I can remember, occurred, not on the leg but at the bottom of the spine. The victim was an in-patient at the RAP and I happened to be there one morning when his ulcer was being dressed. It was the size of a saucer and the backbone was exposed. One orderly was scraping and washing the putrid cavity while another was fanning the air to keep the flies at bay. It was a scene which filled me with helpless pity for the patient and a burning hatred for the callous nation responsible.

Beri-beri and tropical ulcers, plus our traditional enemies, dysentery and malaria which had been endemic since the Mergui days, were the cause of the vast majority of deaths in the 114. On average, members of the British Battalion spent from two to three months in this camp, and during that time thirty nine of them died there, including one of our officers, Lt Wilson of the Sherwood Foresters. His death, which resulted from blackwater fever(a complication of malaria), was the second and last among our twenty officers.

Cholera we were spared, at least in epidemic form. This deadly illness nevertheless occupied our minds a good deal at the 114, partly because the cloudy environment which we experienced there was thought to be conducive to the disease, and partly because there were rumours that a party of British prisoners, brought to the area a year or so previously, from the Bangkok end of the line, had been largely wiped out by it. We had been warned by an MO at Tavoy of the lethal character of cholera. "Make no mistake," he had said, "with this disease you are alive at breakfast time and dead at tea time. So make sure you thoroughly sterilise all your eating and drinking equipment." This dire warning frequently crossed my mind during our mist enshrouded days at the 114 and made me even more anxious to be out of the place.

Towards the end of 1943 there were constant rumours that the Japanese intended shortly to move us to the plains of Thailand where food and medicines would be plentiful and life would be altogether more tolerable, but none of us believed these rumours. Our privation had gone on for so long and had so constantly increased that we found it difficult to imagine any reversal in our fortunes. We were therefore extremely surprised when the move actually began. We were still not convinced that we were necessarily bound for the promised land but we allowed ourselves a degree of cautious optimism based on the fact that we were at least leaving the 114.

We travelled in box wagons on the Railway, in parties of varying size, at irregular intervals, mainly during January. The guard in our wagon told us we were bound for Kanburi_[1] in Thailand. This didn't mean very much to us since our knowledge of the geography of Thailand was extremely sketchy. We knew that Bangkok was the capital but Kanburi we had never heard of. We could only hope therefore that it was a civilised place.

Each wagon carried twenty five prisoners and a guard. We were not therefore too tightly packed, but the wagons, being made of steel, were hot in the daytime and extremely cold at night. We made many stops on the way, sometimes at camp sites to take on rations, or fresh stocks of wood and water for the engine, sometimes at loops in the line to allow trains from the opposite direction to pass us but more often for reasons which were far from clear to us. For most of our journey the track of the Railway followed the course of a river which is now called the Kwai Noi. This river rises on the Burma border and flows southward down the mountains to the Thailand plain where it joins the Kwai Yai. In some places rail and river ran closely parallel, especially where ravines occurred and the passage was narrow. Here the track would sometimes overhang the river, supported on timber stilts built tight against the rock face. In other places where the terrain was more level, the river would completely disappear from our view, concealed by dark green jungle. Sometimes the track crossed deep gorges spanned by tall lattice timbered bridges, peering down from which, as we clanked slowly over them, I felt none too safe. This was partly because the construction of the bridges looked flimsy, and partly because of our obvious

---

[1] *The full name of this town is "Kanchanaburi," but I never heard it referred to other than by its abbreviated name of "Kanburi".*

vulnerability in the event of an air attack. As events turned out, we saw not a single allied aircraft throughout the journey, but it was clear from the broken and overturned trucks which lay at intervals along the track side, that there had been some bombing.

Towards the end of our journey, as we emerged from the jungle, the track crossed an impressive eleven span steel bridge set on concrete piers. The bridge was some two or three hundred yards in length and as we rolled majestically across it the wheels of the train produced a confident metallic rumble which seemed to say that we might, at last, have reached a civilised place. Today, this bridge, which is at Tamarkan, is presented to tourists as "The Bridge Over the River Kwai", as if the fictitious events of the novel and the film of that name had really taken place there. The Tamarkan bridge does span the Kwai(the Kwai Yai to be precise) but otherwise the fiction bears no relation to the events which took place there.

On crossing Tamarkan bridge there wasn't much doubt in our minds that we had reached the Thailand plain. The land was flat, there were houses, there were plots of cultivated land and there was human activity. Kanburi, the journey's end, is less than three miles beyond Tamarkan. We therefore quickly reached it after traversing the bridge. It was a huge camp and as we were shepherded to our billets I saw prisoners of all nationalities. The huts were much the same as we had been used to in Burma, of bamboo and atap construction, but row upon row of them. It grew dark soon after our arrival and the evening meal was served. It was delivered in the usual manner - a bucket of rice and a bucket of stew for each group of fifty or sixty men. The quality of the stew, however, was memorable - thick with vegetables and some pieces of meat in it. I shall never forget that meal. It represented an important turning point in our fortunes, and the result was the saving of many lives which would otherwise have been lost.

Chapter Eight - Kanburi our Mecca

Although the food at Kanburi was remarkably better than in the labour camps of Burma, it was still no more than adequate by any ordinary standards. The greatest improvement was in the quality of the stew we were given at midday and in the evenings. Sometimes the evening meal was further enhanced by the addition of a "doover". This, although in fact nothing more than a savoury rice ball, slightly fried, we considered the height of luxury. Food quantities, however, were never over-generous and the practice of giving us pap for breakfast never changed. The improvement in the diet was nevertheless sufficient to enable many of our sick to recover, especially those who were suffering from beri-beri. Twenty six of the British Battalion, however, who were brought to Kanburi did not recover. Neither did a further eight who, for reasons best known to the Japanese, were deposited at Tamarkan.

Most of the British Battalion deaths at Kanburi occurred in January, shortly after arrival there. These were clearly men whose condition was terminal before leaving the 114. In most cases their lives would have been saved if the move from Burma had been effected a month or two earlier. There was no point in keeping thousands of prisoners in Burma after the completion of the Railway in October 1943, and if the Japanese had had a spark of humanity in their character they would have begun the move to Thailand in that month. Instead, they postponed it for three months and, as a result, deaths in the British Battalion were close on a hundred more than they need have been. This may appear an exaggeration even to survivors, but the figures are as follows;

Deaths prior to 1st November 1943 54

Deaths from 1st November 1943 to 31st March 1944 91

Most of those who died at Kanburi belonged to the army and were not known to me personally. Indeed of the four RAF men who died, I knew only one intimately. This was Reg Bussey, a fellow radar mechanic, who had served with me on stations in both Johore and on Singapore Island. His was a typical case of increasing illness from October 1943, when the Railway was completed, to January 1944 when the move to

Thailand took place. His main problems were beri-beri and malaria and by the time he reached Kanburi he was very ill indeed. I felt he might recover in the improved environment but he faded away towards the end of January. Reg was a gentle soul who did not deserve to be destroyed by war.

LAC Jones was another RAF man whose death at Kanburi I particularly remember, though not because he and I were on any close terms. On the contrary, he was very much a loner, unlike the rest of us who tended to band together in twos and threes. He suffered no significant illness during the building of the Railway, but afterwards his health appeared to collapse dramatically and, by the time he arrived at Kanburi, his condition was serious. At the RAP in Kanburi, where he was an in-patient, he was regularly visited and given eggs, bananas, etc. by another RAF man whose name was Benson. This devotion fascinated me because I knew that normally there was no particular fellowship between the two men. On several occasions, therefore, I asked Benny why he had suddenly become so concerned. Benny at first was evasive but, on being pressed, he eventually said

"Well, the answer's simple enough. We're Masons."

I was rather impressed by this revelation, despite my general aversion to the Masonic movement.

Medical supplies and facilities at Kanburi, though also better than in the jungle camps, were far from adequate, as I found out when I had to have a tooth extracted. A dentist was available but he had no anaesthetic in the shape of either gas or cocaine. He said that if I was willing, he was prepared to inject some aspirin which might deaden the pain.

"How do you inject aspirin?" I asked.

"Well," he said "we just grind up the tablet, mix it with water and put it in the syringe."

"Does it work?" I asked.

"Not always," he replied "but it often helps quite a bit."

I hesitated and was on the point of declining the treatment, especially as the tooth had now ceased to ache, when the dentist said.

"Well look, let me give you the injection. See if it takes, then make up your mind."

This seemed reasonable and I said "OK".

A medical orderly standing at a nearby bench, then began to prepare the injection. During this procedure a second medical orderly strolled in, sidled up to his friend, and asked

"How much are you giving them?"

"About half a tablet," said the other in a low voice, "but this bugger'll be lucky if he gets a third."

The prospect of an inadequate dose of dubious anaesthetic alarmed me and my first impulse was to make a bolt for it but, recalling that I had the option of not proceeding if the injection proved ineffective, I sat tight, though not with any great confidence.

The concoction was mixed and the loaded syringe was handed to the dentist. He came over to the high stool on which I was seated. I opened my mouth and in went the needle. The pain was excruciating.

"I'll leave you for a few minutes," he said, "and we'll see how things go."

With that he went out. I hoped the anaesthetic would gradually quell the pain, but it did not. On the contrary, the pain grew worse, clearly demonstrating that the aspirin was useless, if not positively harmful.

"Well," said the dentist, on returning, "how goes it?"

"It hasn't worked," I said "and the tooth aches like hell."

The dentist plucked my cheek, stood back and looked at me, then said

"Well now, shall I take it out or leave it in?"

"It'll have to come out," I replied, "I'm in agony."

"Right," he said, "stand up a minute."

143

I did so and he turned the stool on which I had been sitting, onto its side. He then motioned me to sit down again on what was now a somewhat precarious perch of greatly reduced height. The purpose of this adjustment was no doubt to ensure maximum power and leverage, an objective which, though laudable enough in itself, engendered in me a feeling of extreme vulnerability as I re-seated myself.

The dentist, armed with forceps, now positioned himself to operate. He stood close to my right side and pressed the inside of his left leg against my back. He pushed my head backwards. I opened my mouth with some reluctance and, putting his free hand on my shoulder, he took a firm grip of the offending molar with his forceps. Then came the first wrench, towards one side. There was a cracking sound as if bone were being splintered, and intense pain. Then, immediately, the cracking sound again and more pain, as he levered mercilessly in the opposite direction. Then, again without pause, a final shaft of agony as the tooth was lifted clear of its socket. The dentist gave the evacuated gum a professional squeeze between his thumb and forefinger and the torture was over. I groaned with relief, leaned forward and spat a mouthful of blood onto the bare earth floor.

"OK?" queried the dentist, giving my shoulder a fatherly squeeze.

"Yes," I replied, not too firmly. "Thanks."

"Right," he said, helping me to my feet, "now don't eat anything on that side of your mouth for the next twenty four hours. Keep off hot liquids as well and, if you have any trouble, come and see me again."

I did have some trouble but I did not go back to the dentist. The first problem was bleeding, which did not stop for twenty four hours. The second was a splinter of tooth left in the gum. This made its presence felt some weeks after the extraction but I managed to dig it out myself.

My impression generally, as regards dental problems on the Railway, is that they were a rarity. I cannot recall any other prisoner experiencing a rotten tooth and, apart from the incident described, I had no such problems myself.

The dental episode at Kanburi was my worst experience at that camp. Otherwise, life there was tolerable, indeed rather dull especially as, for some weeks after our arrival, there were no working parties and we thus spent all our time within the confines of the camp. During this period, perhaps to relieve the tedium, the Japanese announced a campaign to rid the camp of rats. We were to catch as many as possible and would be given ten cents for every tail produced. It seemed at first an attractive offer but we quickly discovered that, having no traps, it was extremely difficult to capture the creatures. I caught none at all and quickly lost all enthusiasm, but then, quite unexpectedly, I came across a nest with six young rats in it. These I delivered, pink and wriggling to the British orderly room and claimed sixty cents. Doubt was expressed as to the eligibility of the bag and I had to wait twenty four hours while the matter was referred to the Japanese. The next day, when I went back to the orderly room, I was told that judgement had been given in my favour and I was duly paid the sixty cents, but I was warned that the decision was not to be taken as a precedent!

The freedom from work was a blessing in the sense that it helped many of us to recover from our various ailments. In my case I was particularly pleased to note the rapid disappearance of the beri-beri swellings from my legs. No work, however, meant no pay and, without money, nothing could be bought from the excellent canteen. This did not greatly trouble me so far as foodstuffs were concerned, the ration being sufficient for survival, but I did need tobacco, stocks having become dangerously low despite stringent economy measures such as smoking less, rolling the cigarettes ever more thinly, and reusing butt ends. However, always the darkest hour before the dawn! I was contemplating the misery of a smokeless future when I happened to fall into conversation with a Dutch lieutenant. Pleasantries were exchanged and, when I felt the moment was ripe, I made a casual reference to my shortage of the vital weed. This brought forth not only the offer of an immediate smoke(which I gladly accepted) but also the suggestion that I might like to teach the lieutenant English in return for as many cigarettes as I cared to roll during the lessons. I accepted the offer eagerly and without much thought, not realising until later that free smokes in the evenings, which was when the lessons were to be given, was not the complete answer to my problem. However, the lessons began that same evening, in the hut where the lieutenant was housed along with a number of fellow officers of the Dutch army.

Our text was an American crime novel. This was not the ideal type of literature on which to base a study of the English language, but it was the only book the lieutenant had and it therefore had to suffice. Almost every sentence in it contained either a grammatical liberty, a spelling variation, a slang word which needed translation or an expression which did not have the same meaning in England as in the United States. It was necessary, for example, to explain the difference between being "knocked up" in New York and being "knocked up" in London. Bogged down with these complications I quickly began to find teaching very tiresome. I also became increasingly annoyed at the lieutenant's constant reference to his Prussian military ancestry. He didn't seem at all aware that most people regarded Prussian influence as the basic cause of Germany's aggressive history. However, in order to preserve my only means of obtaining tobacco, it was essential to persevere with the lessons, and I did so.

During the lessons, we relied for light on a crudely constructed oil lamp which belonged to the lieutenant. It consisted of a round shallow tin filled with oil and a rag wick clamped in a double length of iron wire fixed across the top of the tin. Although the poor light from this device made it difficult to read our text, it gave me, every time I rolled a cigarette, the opportunity of filching, unseen, some extra tobacco for later use. This was accomplished by concealing the extra tobacco in the palm of the hand beneath the second, third and fourth fingers, then surreptitiously transferring it at a convenient moment to the pockets of my shorts. The system worked very well and after a week or so I began to accumulate quite a useful stock. There was fortunately no risk of detection by reference to any diminution of the lieutenant's stock, because the amount of tobacco he had was so huge. An indication of the size of his stock may be judged from the fact that he kept it in a large biscuit tin about a foot square. I relate this tale not out of pride in my skill at theft, but to demonstrate the fragility of moral values in the face of dire need.

Early in February 1944 we were all given another postcard to send home. The front of the card was headed "Service des Prisonniers de Guerre" and on the back, underneath the legend "Imperial Japanese Army", the following message was printed.

"Our present place, quarters and work is unchanged since last card sent to you. The rains have finished, it is now beautiful weather. I am working healthily (sick). We receive newspapers printed in English which reveal world events."

"We have joyfully received a present of some milk, tea, margarine, sugar and cigarettes from Japanese Authorities."

"We are very anxious to hear from home, but some prisoners have received letters or cables."

"Every one is hopeful of a speedy end to the war and with faith in the future we look forward to a happy reunion soon."

"With best wishes for a cheerful Christmas."

I was not particularly concerned about the accuracy of this message. If the card reached home it would indicate that I was still alive and that was all I wanted. It is interesting, nevertheless, that, at the time of sending these cards, we had not seen a newspaper for six months, nor did the Japanese ever give us any of the listed "presents" apart from occasional small quantities of sugar. The Christmas greeting was also out of date, owing no doubt to frustrated plans for earlier despatch of the cards.

Also in February, we received Red Cross parcels. This event amazed us, nothing whatever having previously reached us from that source. The parcels were about eighteen inches square and nine inches deep, and contained foodstuffs from the United States. I recall particularly the powdered milk and the coffee. There were also Camel cigarettes. Unfortunately each parcel had to be shared by five prisoners, which meant that individual portions were small, but we were very lucky

147

compared with many other camps where, we learned later, each parcel had had to be shared among as many as twenty five men. As this was the first time the Japanese had allowed anything to reach us from the Red Cross, we thought it might be a sign that the war was turning in our favour and that our captors were attempting to improve their heavily tarnished image, but as the months passed and no further parcels were received, some doubt was cast on this theory.

It had been strongly rumoured even before we left Burma that, on completion of the Railway, we would be transferred to Japan. We were not therefore particularly surprised when, during March 1994, it was announced that those considered fit were to be taken by land to Saigon and thence by sea to the Land of the Rising Sun. Many of the prisoners hoped to be chosen, but I did not. It was a very long sea journey to Japan and there seemed to me a considerable risk of being sunk on the way by Allied forces. My strategy was therefore to present myself at the selection parade looking as sickly as possible. In this respect I had circumstances on my side to a great extent. I was normally of slim build, and ever since the dysentery attack at Mergui I had been even thinner than usual, all ribs being still plainly countable despite the improved rations at Kanburi. This head start in the matter of appearance I was able to further enhance by wearing at the parade only a gee string and a threadbare blanket. I wore the blanket draped from suitably hunched shoulders and kept it sufficiently open at the front for the ribs to be observable. I had bare feet, my hair was close cropped and I assumed as miserable a facial expression as I could muster.

The judgement, fit or sick, was given by a single Japanese soldier who sat at a desk in the middle of the parade ground. We formed in a long line and, in turn, we each stood in front of the desk. First there was an anal examination. This was carried out by a second Japanese soldier who required us to bend over and submit to the insertion of a glass rod. I am not certain exactly what the purpose of this was. However, not having experienced a solid motion for close on two years, I was hopeful of failing this test. The rod was inserted, withdrawn and scrutinised. The glass rod operator spoke a few words to the man at the desk who surveyed me for a moment or two and then motioned me to the group of "unacceptables". This was gratifying, though whether I failed on both the anal and the visual examination, or only one of the tests, I shall never know. Not that I greatly cared. I was not going to Japan and of that I was mighty glad.

About a hundred and twenty men of the British Battalion were selected for Japan and about twice as many were rejected - a ratio which speaks for itself as regards our state of health as a whole. On completion of the selection process, the chosen were immediately marched out of the camp and I heard nothing more of them until the end of the war when, on the homeward journey, I met some of them again and they gave me the following account.

From Kanburi they went to Tamarkan, where they joined a large group of Dutch, Australian and American prisoners who were also destined for Japan. They were inoculated and issued with new clothing, then put on the train for Saigon. Here they remained until the end of the war. Why the sea journey to Japan never took place is unclear, but it appears that owing to increasing Japanese reverses in the war, the necessary shipping never became available. A more charitable view would be that the Japanese came to the conclusion that sea transport of prisoners had become too dangerous, but such a theory hardly fits the Japanese character.

At Saigon, the living conditions were vastly superior to anything the prisoners had previously experienced: brick built accommodation, running water, electric light, a varied diet, regular rest days with organised entertainment and sport, issues of clothing from time to time and gifts, including food and musical instruments, from the French Red Cross. These conditions were apparently the result of the Vichy style government which the Japanese had set up in Indo China. Although the French by no means had absolute authority, they did retain some control. Also, perhaps more importantly, the French had freedom of movement. The Japanese, in effect, were thus under constant surveillance and this no doubt influenced their treatment of the prisoners.

The British Battalion at Saigon suffered only one death, that of T H Ryan, an able seaman of the Royal Navy. It was a tragic death caused inadvertently by a fellow prisoner. The two men were shovelling some rubbish when a rat suddenly appeared. They both went for the rat with their shovels and in the excitement of the moment Ryan's thumb was struck by the other man's shovel. Tetanus developed and quickly proved fatal. I did not discover the true facts of this event until forty years afterwards when, at a reunion, I happened to raise the matter of Ryan's death with a fellow ex-prisoner. Up to this time the story I had was that Ryan had accidentally stuck a fork through his boot and injured a toe, thus causing the fatal tetanus. Indeed, I had given this story to Ryan's mother who, at the end of the war, had written to me for information on the circumstances of her son's death. The man I now met at the reunion gave me the revised story and, since he said it was his shovel which had struck the mortal blow, I have no reason to doubt it. It was a matter which clearly had weighed heavily on his conscience for many years and he was full of self condemnation. I tried to convince him that there was no reason to reproach himself but nothing I said was of any effect. I felt deeply sorry for him and for that reason I feel he should remain anonymous.

Shortly after the departure of the Japan party, those of us who remained at Kanburi were assigned to various working parties. The party to which I was attached was about twenty strong and its function was hut building on a site about a mile away from the camp. At first we were chiefly involved in preparation of the site - clearing trees and shrubs, levelling the land and digging post holes. Later on we were engaged on transporting timber and other materials by lorry from a supply dump in the town, sawing the timber on site and generally assisting the Japanese army engineers who were building the huts. It was easy work, especially by comparison with our experiences in Burma, and we had the unusual advantage of a considerate Japanese sergeant in charge of us. He was civil and he was easy-going. He allowed us a long lunch beak and several generous additional breaks throughout the day. During one of those breaks, on our first morning with him. he surprised us by buying some water melons, slicing them in segments, and giving us a piece each. They were delicious - huge ear to ear slices of succulent red fruit which we consumed with great gusto. In the afternoon we were further surprised by a repetition of this performance. More water melon slices, which we again consumed with great relish. Noting our obvious enjoyment, the sergeant asked "You likee-ga?" "Ga", I should mention, or sometimes "ka", is the suffix which apparently in the Japanese language turns a statement into a question, and the Japanese often used it even when putting a question in English.

"You likee-ga? queried the sergeant, smiling broadly.

"Yes. Very good," we chorused. Then one of our number suggested "Tomorrow, again. OK?"

"Nai, nai," replied the sergeant, gravely shaking his head and marching off. But on the following day the sergeant did again buy us melons, both in the morning and the afternoon. And he continued to provide us with melons twice a day for the rest of the time he was in charge of us.

When it became clear that the daily melon giving had become established practice, we asked the sergeant why he was so generous. He said that, at the outbreak of war, his wife had been in Australia. She had been interned for a time and then been repatriated on an internee exchange scheme. On arriving back in Japan she had reported kindly treatment by the Australians and he was therefore anxious to reciprocate. It was a touching story. It demonstrated that, even among the Japanese, there were individuals who were capable of human kindness - at least on a reciprocal basis.

By our standards the gift of the water melons was a trivial gesture but, viewed against the harsh life and outlook of the Japanese soldiery, it was a considerable act of charity. It is seldom realised in our country just how tough the life of a Japanese soldier was. He was required to fight to the death in all circumstances and discipline was enforced by "fist law", which meant that the slightest infringement of the regulations was punishable by a beating. At its mildest, this took the form of slaps and punches to the head which the offender was not allowed to resist. Add to this the Japanese propaganda which taught all its soldiers that they were engaged in a war to free southern Asia from the wicked white imperialists, and Japan's ill treatment of its prisoners becomes more understanable. In their eyes we were wicked because we were white imperialists, and we were contemptible because we had hoisted the white flag. I often think about the deep emotional shock which must have struck the Japanese nation when, on the instructions of their god-emperor(no less), they themselves finally had to surrender. The trauma must have been hard to bear and no doubt, in many Japanese, engendered a deep desire for eventual revenge. To what extent that desire persists today remains a disturbingly unanswered question.

Kanburi remains in my memory chiefly as the camp where my confidence in survival was restored. We had sufficient to eat, there was no heavy labour and the environment, compared with the jungle camps, seemed civilised and safe. Even the weather was on our side. It was the dry season and my limited wardrobe was therefore adequate. There was, however, one recurrent problem - a shortage of wood for the cookhouse fires. In the jungle camps we had simply cut down a tree or a clump of bamboo as necessary, but at Kanburi the wood had to be bought by the Japanese from local traders and transported to the camp. It frequently did not arrive, and when this happened meals were either delayed or cancelled. Rumour had it that the camp commandant was selling our wood and pocketing the proceeds, but whether or not this was so there was no means of telling. I don't think the problem caused any loss of rations, the tendency being to deal out a bumper serving when a meal had been missed. It did, however, cause some anxiety at times, and a great deal of annoyance.

There was at Kanburi a certain amount of apprehension about the risk from Allied air raids. The sound of large numbers of aircraft flying high overhead at night had become commonplace, and there had been instances of daylight raids at various places on the Railway. We were therefore on the qui vive and ready to dive into the nearest monsoon drain if it looked as if we might be threatened. This fact was behind a rather unkind joke which was played on Stan Vaisey. It was noon and Stan was lying on his back in his hut, snoozing. A group of lads came into the hut for their midday break and one of them bellowed into Stan's ear

"Quick, Stan, get you head down."

Stan sprang upright in alarm but, hearing no aircraft, petulantly enquired

"What's up, for Christ's sake? What's up?"

"They're looking for wood for the cookhouse fires," replied his tormentor.

Stan's trenchant response is, regrettably, unprintable.

After spending some four or five months at Kanburi, I began to assume that I would end the war there, but towards the end of May(1944) I was detailed to join a party destined for railway work up country. This was a considerable shock which made me feel that I might have been better off on the Japan party. Before we left, there was a limited kit issue. Most of the articles involved were second hand clothes and blankets, and the quantities were small. The majority of us consequently obtained nothing but I was given a shirt, having pleaded strongly that I had been without one for eighteen months. The garment I received was of grey cotton and in fairly good condition - certainly better condition than my shorts, which now consisted largely of green patches held precariously together by all too little of the original khaki material. If I could have got a pair of boots as well I would have considered myself fully equipped but, although a few pairs of boots were available, they were mainly in sizes which were too small.

Also prior to my departure from Kanburi, I sent off my fourth and last postcard. It was dated 19th May 1944 and its printed message (designed for deletions and additions as appropriate) read as follows:

"Your mails (and   ) are received with thanks.

My health is (good, usual, poor).

I am ill in hospital.

I am working for pay (I am paid monthly salary).

I am not working.

My best regards to...

Yours ever

...."

Purposely designed, no doubt, to reveal nothing significant the card succeeded admirably in that respect. Even so, I was glad to be able to send it - for the same reason as before, namely that, if it arrived(which it did) it would at least indicate my continued survival.

We left Kanburi towards the end of May, trundling northward in box wagons on the Railway. The monsoon rains were due to begin shortly and this prospect, coupled with thoughts of life in a jungle camp, depressed me considerably. Our destination was Indato, which it took us some twelve hours to reach. It was ninety miles from Kanburi and about sixty miles from the border with Burma.

Chapter Nine - Back on the Railway

On arrival at Indato we were shepherded to a hut which was already partly occupied by Americans. The hut, of normal bamboo and atap construction, appeared to be new but had no sleeping platforms. The Americans had therefore built themselves bunks and we set about providing ourselves with similar accommodation. There wasn't room for single bunks. Most of them we therefore built as "doubles", one above the other. Bamboo poles, lashed together with wire or rope or similar material, were used for the framework of the bunks and rice sacks, stretched across the framework, formed the bed - except in the case of Macdougall, my co-constructor, who used what he called his bullet proof sheet to form his bed. This was a large and ancient waterproof sheet which time and the tropics had caused to perish and stiffen out of all recognition. Its waterproof quality had long since been destroyed and it had come to resemble more a board than a sheet. It could no longer be folded. It had to be bent and, on being unpacked, had to be unbent and beaten flat before it could be used, but despite these limitations it was still strong and continued to serve well as the basic component of Mac's bed construction kit.

Having completed our dual bunk, Mac and I went outside to explore the environment. It was depressingly familiar: a parade ground surrounded by huts. On the far side of the parade ground our eye was caught by the glimmer of the cookhouse fires and we strolled across to take a look. Again the customary scene: a row of low-built fireplaces with a bubbling kuali on each. One of the kualis contained a none-too-thick looking stew, the others rice. Clearly, the standard meal was in course of preparation. We continued our ramble, noting on the way the presence of Australians and some more Americans. Beyond the last of the huts, in a slight depression on the far edge of the camp, we came upon what appeared to have been a cultivated patch of bananas. The area was fast reverting to jungle but some four or five plantains were still growing there and one of them bore a promising stem of bananas. The fruit was still green but it was well developed and we decided to have it. It was eight or nine feet above ground level and to get it we had to break the plantain off about half way up. This we did by swinging on it. We then broke off the stem of bananas from the top of the plantain and carried it back to our hut. How many bananas were on the stem I do not know, we did not count them, but there must have been a hundred. We stowed them under our dual bunk hoping they would eventually ripen and provide us with a useful supplement to our rice and stew diet. Not surprisingly, our arrival with the fruit did not go unnoticed. Enquiries came from all sides as to where it had been procured. We told our story, including the fact that there were no more bananas worth picking, but one or two of our confreres nevertheless disappeared for a time, obviously determined to check out the prospects for themselves. When they came back empty handed it occurred to me that we might well have difficulty in guarding our prize.

Although, as I have said, the majority of bunks which we built were two tier contrivances, three of our number decided to go one better by building a triple decker. The men involved in this high rise project were Matelot Wright (a gunner), Geordie Ross(also a gunner) and Billy Cooper, an able seaman. They duly completed the structure and, with obvious pride, stood back to admire their handiwork. It was undoubtedly a splendid edifice, its top tier standing proudly above the more modest efforts of the rest of us. Matelot climbed into the bottom bunk, then Geordie into the second and Billy into the top. Billy had some difficulty in getting to the top of the structure. This was partly because he couldn't stop laughing, but he eventually reached his objective and flung himself, somewhat heavily, onto the topmost bunk. There was a noise like the sound of several rapid rifle shots as the bamboo poles supporting Billy gave way and deposited him with considerable force onto Geordie beneath. After a moment's pause, the bamboo supporting Geordie similarly collapsed depositing both Billy and Geordie onto the luckless Matelot. There was a moment or two of dreadful silence before the three of them began to extricate themselves from the tangled wreckage. Billy began to chuckle again, but Matelot, who had endured the full weight of both his comrades, was far from amused. He held Billy responsible for the catastrophe and grumbled for a long time. I cannot remember whether they rebuilt their triple decker or replaced it with a single and a double. I do recall that none of them was seriously injured.

At Indato I became particularly friendly with one of the Americans with whom we shared the hut. This was Salvador Pitchon, a striker who had survived the sinking of the USS Houston. "Striker", I should explain, is the American expression for a telegraphist. Salvador was over six feet tall, Jewish and came from the Bronx. His father was a Turk and his mother Cuban. Most of his fellow Americans were from the southern states and several of them had the habit of baiting Pitchon on his Jewishness. His most persistent tormentor was a scrawny little black haired youth from Kentucky whose typically opening remark would be:

"Ah tell yer Pitchon, if ah had mah way, I'd put all the fuckin' Jews again a wall and I'd shoot 'em down like dorgs."

I was never able to decide whether such insults represented a genuine hatred of Jews or whether they were designed simply to inflame a susceptible subject and make sport of him. Certainly, when goaded in this way, Pitchon always reacted very quickly, going immediately for his persecutor with his fists. Allowed a fair fight, he would undoubtedly have made mincemeat of the Kentucky tyke, but the latter had too many supporters who inevitably came to his assistance. Pitchon was consequently always the loser in such battles and often suffered quite a bruising. Witnessing these events, and not having previously met any Americans, I wondered what sort of a nation they were. Those I met at Indato were certainly a mixed bunch. Many had their roots in the various European countries, but there was also a half-Japanese among them and a Red Indian called Snake. There were also three Mexicans. Two of them, Rodriquez and Martinez, were lithe and bronzed and the third, Pete Mendoza, was thick set, black and moustachioed. Not having been taught at school any American history beyond 1783, I was unaware of the vast racial mix of that country. It therefore came to my notice as a considerable surprise.

Most of our work at Indato consisted of digging and carrying earth for the repair of embankments at various points along the railway, where slippage had occured. Tha Japanese did not, however, put anything like the pressure on us that they had done during the comstruction of the line. Nor was the weather as bad as I had expected. There was rain at times but we did not suffer the constant deluge which we had experienced during the wet season in Burma. There was nevertheless, some flooding, particularly on the road which we regularly used on our way to and from work. At one point on this road we regularly had to wade knee deep for some twenty or thirty yards.

Those who were fortunate enough to own petrol cans at Indato did not have to labour on the railway, they accompanied the working parties but spent the day boiling water for the workers to drink. I did not own a can, but Pitchon did, he consequently had a permanent place as a water boiler. One morning, owing to a bout of malaria, he was unable to join the working party and I therefore asked him if I could borrow the petrol can in order to get on the water boiling detail. He was reluctant at first, but on my solemnly promising to guard the can with my life, he let me have it. Off I went, delighted. On arrival at the work site, I duly attached myself to the small band of water boilers.

The first task of this select group was to fetch water from the nearby river. This we did in tandem pairs, each couple carrying two or three four gallon cans, hung by their wire handles from a bamboo pole supported on the shoulders. The bank of the river sloped steeply down to the water and was muddy from recent rain. My partner and I, both with bare feet, had some difficulty in clambering up this slimy incline, and about half way up, I slipped and went down on one knee, causing the can nearest to me to strike the ground with some force. We paused for a minute or two, adjusted the cans on the pole, and were about to resume the climb when I noticed that one of the cans was half empty.. I looked it over and found that it was holed at one of its corners. I also realised that the damaged can was Pitchon's, a dreadful discovery which caused me to spend the rest of the day feverishly wondering how on earth I was going to break the awful news to Pitchon, and I still had not solved my problem by the time we returned to camp. I therefore approached the sick man's bunk with considerable reluctance.

Pitchon looked very pale, and I thought how unfit he was to receive bad news.

"How are you ?" I asked.

"Lousy" he replied. "Sweating all day and sick. Is my can ok?"

I was taken aback by such a pointed enquiry so early in our discourse and, inevitably, I hesitated in my reply. This was fatal. He instantly became suspicious, and put his question again.

"My can is ok, isn't it ?"

"Well" I replied, fumbling for some form of words which might soften the blow, "No".

I got no further.

"Goddam" exploded Pitchon, "You busted mah can!"

"Well yes" I said. "We had an accident, and there's a hole in it"

"Jesus Christ! Jesus Christ! Jesus Christ!" moaned Pitchon, in deep despair, hand clapped to brow and shaking his head from side to side in time with the oath (which incidentally, I thought particularly inappropriate in his case).

"I told you specifically to take care of the dam' can and here you've busted it", he grumbled

"I know," I replied, "and I'm damn sorry, but I'll pay for it to be mended"

"Can it be mended?" he asked

"O yes " I said, "I think so" I was not in fact at all certain that it could, but I felt bound to appear as optimistic as possible.

His gloom lifted slightly.

"I sure hope it can be fixed" he said, "Its a goddam valuable thing"

"Yes" I said "I know, and I'll certainly see what can be done".

In most of the prisoner of war camps there was generally at least one tinsmith to be found, and at Indato he was an Australian. I located him in the cookhouse, where men of his trade were frequently to be found, mending, maintaining, and adapting the various culinary vessels. Using only the most basic of tools, often nothing more than a hammer, and certainly never anything as sophisticated as a soldering iron the tinsmiths worked metalic miracles on a wide range of tin cans and steel drums.

The Australian quoted me seventy-five cents to repair Pitchon's can. This was a rather large sum against the wage level at the time. I therefore had to defer the job until pay day at the end of the month, and when I reported the position to Pitchon I got the impression that he felt I intended to renege. It was not therefore until pay day had passed and the can had been repaired as promised, that our friendship was fully restored. Pitchon subsequently suffered several more crippling bouts of malaria, but I never again asked to borrow the precious can.

Our hoard of bananas remained stubbornly green for a long time but eventually a few of them turned yellowish and these we cut from the stem for less conspicuous storage in our haversacks. Being eager to improve our diet at the earliest opportunity, we ate many of this first "cut" before they were fully ripe. But there was no shortage of yellowing bananas from the stem and before long we found ourselves short of storage space for the final ripening process. We kept the haversacks constantly full and the overflow went into blanket roles, under pillows and into various other nooks and crannies. The supply lasted for several weeks, during which time we were consuming four or five bananas each, every day. In fact, at the end. we were rather tired of the monotonous diet.

After a week or two of railway repair work, I found myself one morning detailed to fell timber. There were about half a dozen of us and the site was a mile or so from the camp. Our job was to cut down the trees, trim them and load the trunks onto a lorry. It was strenuous work and my glasses had kept slipping down my sweaty nose. I had therefore taken them off and put them on the ground in my upturned straw hat. The lorry arrived for loading and backed slowly towards the heap of logs. Too late I realised that the rear wheel of the vehicle was about to pass over the hat and glasses. And it did. In fact, if the driver had been purposely aiming at the hat he couldn't have hit it more squarely. Relentlessly, the great wheel crunched slowly across the hat and its precious contents. It was a moment of helpless despair and angry self-reproach. Why on earth had I put the glasses in such a vulnerable place? I picked up the flattened hat and examined the glasses, expecting them to be crushed to pieces, but they were not. They were whole. I put them on, half expecting them to disintegrate, but they did not. They were quite definitely undamaged. It seemed that a miracle had been wrought, but I then remembered that the rear wheels of the lorry were double. I therefore presume that it was the gap between the two tyres which passed over the glasses, thus exerting no pressure. I was not so concerned about the hat but it too, following some manipulation, proved serviceable.

There is a well known saying in the British armed forces: "never volunteer for anything", but at Indato I ignored this maxim when volunteers were called for to work at the local Japanese army hospital. There was no information on the type of work involved, but I felt it was unlikely to be any worse than navvying on the railway, and I therefore offered my services.

There were six of us and we travelled the short distance to the hospital by train. I say "by train", but "by locomotive" would be more accurate since, when the train arrived, all its trucks were found to be full and we were told to climb onto the engine. This, I thought, would be fun but I quickly changed my mind when, having clambered up, I was met by the huge heat from the boiler. Along the length of the boiler there ran a handrail but it was too hot to be held continuously. I therefore had to cling onto it first with one hand then with the other. It was a precarious ride and I was much relieved when it ended.

The medical officer in charge of the hospital was a major, who proved to be the most civilised Japanese I ever met. He had travelled in both England and America and spoke English, French and German. He was familiar with the works of Shakespeare and made great effort to discuss them with us, but unfortunately his knowledge of the subject was far greater than ours and we therefore made very little headway. I did my best with my limited grammar school knowledge of the bard but I found myself all too quickly out of my depth.

The Major gave all of us a daily dose of quinine as a. precaution against malaria, and also as much Japanese officers' toilet paper as we wanted. He was highly amused when we explained that the toilet paper was for rolling cigarettes and that any surplus which we might acquire could be profitably disposed of.

Our midday meals at the hospital were also memorable. They consisted of rice and stew, as in the camp, but the difference was in the quality of the stew. It was thick with meat and vegetables and, best of all, we were not limited to a single helping. On returning to the camp, which we did each evening, the contrast in the food was depressing.

Our work at the hospital was chiefly gardening, with an occasional spell in the kitchen, cleaning and peeling vegetables. The gardening consisted of cutting away the scrub which surrounded the hospital, digging the land and sowing various vegetable seeds. The soil was perfect for crop growing - black, fertile and loamy, but unfortunately weeds grew equally well in it and very soon we had to stop extending the plot in order to deal with them. At the end of the three or four weeks which we spent at the hospital we nevertheless had two rows of excellent spring onions, all growing splendidly. If the job had lasted longer, and the onions had matured, we would no doubt have had a share of them by fair means or foul but word came that the work at Indato was finished and that we were all to be taken back to Kanburi. This news I received with mixed feelings. Base camp life generally was preferable to an up country existence, but Indato hospital had been an exception.

Chapter Ten - Duck Farming at Tamarkan

Our train of box wagons rumbled slowly and sonorously across the steel bridge at Tamarkan and, having cleared it, came to a squeaking halt. I assumed that the pause would be brief and that we would shortly move forward again, journeys on the Burma Railway being always heavily punctuated by inexplicable stoppages, but after a minute or two we were told to detrain and, on doing so, were marched into the nearby Tamarkan prison camp.

Tamarkan was smaller than Kanburi but otherwise very similar: drab rows of bamboo huts with a parade ground at the centre. It lay in one of the right-angles formed by the river and the Railway which ran across it. It was approximately oblong in shape and one of its shorter sides was hard against a shallow cutting in which ran what had been the original line of the Railway. This line, which traversed the river by a wooden bridge, was now disused, having been replaced by a loop line running across the steel bridge. Beyond the steel bridge loop there was an antiaircraft gun site equipped with four 4.5 inch guns which the Japanese had captured from the British. From the corner of the prison camp which lay in the right-angle formed by the river and the railway, the longer side of the camp diverged away from the river and, in the triangle of land between the camp and the river the Japanese had their quarters, separated from the prison camp by a dirt road.

The gun site, I guess, was about two hundred yards from the camp perimeter. It was not visible from the camp, owing to intervening trees, but we were quickly made aware of its presence when it opened fire on allied bombers flying overhead. This occurred on our first night at the camp and on many nights subsequently. If one happened to be awake and aware of the approach of the aircraft, the subsequent crash of the guns was not such a shock, but if one happened to be wakened by the guns opening fire it was a frightening experience, especially as, at times, the blast from the guns would ripple one's blanket.

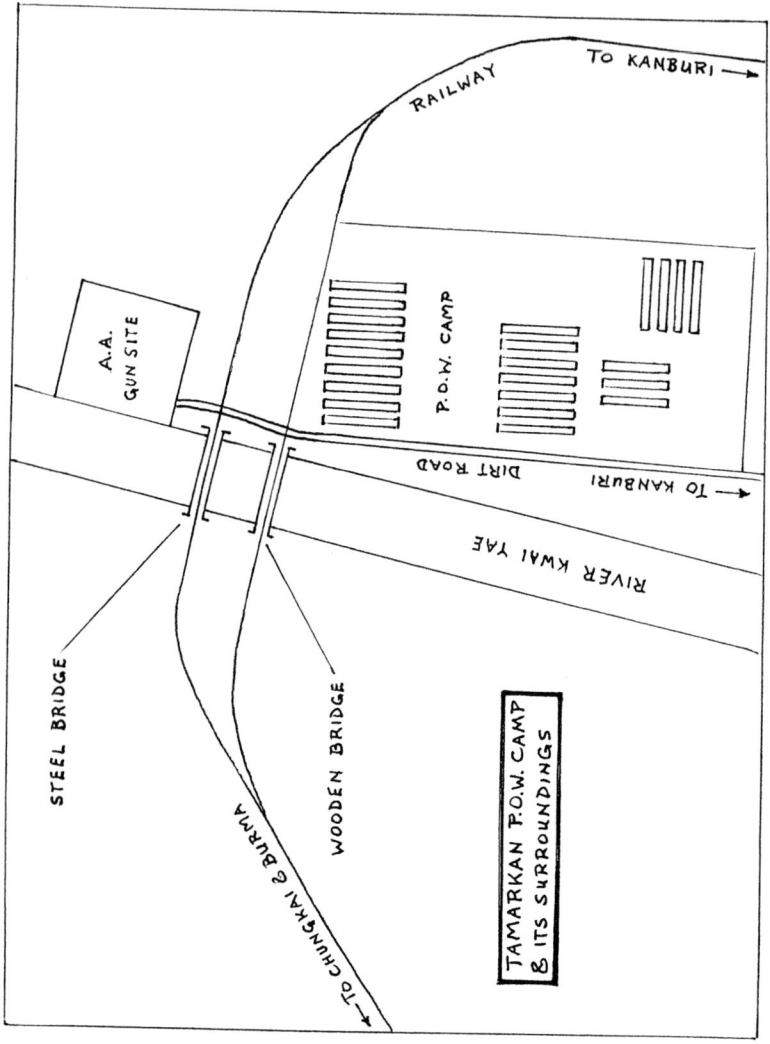

Figure 30 - Map of Tamarkan prison camp

The British contingent from Indato was unfortunately housed in one of the row of huts which ran parallel to the camp perimeter nearest the gun site. We therefore suffered maximum exposure to the noise of the guns and many were the curses of my comrades. "Those buggers 'll bang off just once too often one of these nights and get us all bombed to hell," was a typical comment. In fact the night bombers never did attack us, but the risk of such an attack remained a constant fear in our minds. Looking back over the years, I doubt if there was any great risk that the night bombers would attack the gun site. From the height at which they flew, they probably regarded the antiaircraft fire as harmless. They no doubt had much more important targets to attack and I doubt if it ever crossed the minds of the aircrew involved to bother with the Tamarkan gun site. Our viewpoint, however, was different. We were on the ground, involved in the noise of the guns, and we naturally felt vulnerable.

Conditions generally at Tamarkan were comparatively good. Rations, though not liberal, were sufficient for survival and there was a well stocked canteen for those who had the wherewithal. We were also regularly entertained by a concert party. The performers were mainly Australian and the shows they gave reminded me of English holiday entertainment on the pier. First there was the opening chorus. This involved the whole company in line abreast across the stage, singing and leg wagging to a catchy little melody. This was followed by a series of variety acts. There was comedy, often involving female roles grotesquely portrayed, some burlesque based on life and personalities in the camp, and there were various solo performances, both vocal and instrumental. The audience was invited to join in some of the better known songs and, in this connection, I particularly recall "On the Road to Mandalay". Bearing in mind the limited facilities and the shortage of materials especially for costumes it is remarkable that such shows were produced so successfully, but the company were surprisingly resourceful and the entertainment which they regularly presented was widely appreciated.

A more sombre aspect of Tamarkan was the limbless prisoners. There were at least fifty of them. They were housed together in a hut near ours and each morning they were paraded for a bathe in the river. Most of them had lost a leg. All had undergone primitive amputations in the jungle and, in the sense that they had survived this horrific experience, I suppose they were lucky. They were nevertheless a piteous band and as I watched them each morning, labouring their way towards the river, on their creaking bamboo crutches, I thought how fortunate I was that I still had two sound legs on which to walk and work, despite having suffered tropical ulcers which might well have become gangrenous and led to a similar fate.

Having two sound legs at Tamarkan, however, was no guarantee of paid work. There was a dearth of such employment and I counted myself lucky therefore to be drafted to the gardening party which did attract a wage. The work was similar to that at Indato hospital but on a much bigger scale and employing many more prisoners. The plot was in the triangle of land between the camp and the river and each morning we were issued with tools for the job from a large shed in the Japanese compound. One morning, as we lined up at the shed, I saw at the unglazed window of one of the nearby huts, a Korean private and a Japanese officer. The Korean was standing stiffly to attention and the Japanese officer was clearly berating him for some misdemeanour. As the reprimand proceeded, the officer became increasingly angry. His voice rose to a scream and eventually, completely beside himself, he struck the Korean a massive two handed blow on the top of the head with the flat of his sheathed sword. The Korean dropped out of sight, apparently stunned, and I expected at this juncture that the officer's anger. having been vented to a great extent, would subside, but no such luck. He stood over the fallen man, brandishing his sword and screaming with increased passion. After a moment or two, the head of the Korean reappeared unsteadily above the windowsill, only to be struck another fearsome blow which again knocked the man to the ground. This was repeated several times. As often as the Korean came up, so he was knocked down. It was like a human performance of Punch and Judy, and the show was still going on when we were marched away to the garden. Later enquiries, however, elicited the information that the officer had eventually dragged the Korean to the door of the hut, flung him down a flight of steps and then repeatedly jumped on him, eventually killing him.

This episode of the Japanese officer and the Korean private sickened me. It confirmed my feeling that the Japanese were fundamentally a primitive and vicious people. It also demonstrated the contempt in which the Koreans were held by their Japanese colonial masters. At a later camp, towards the end of the war, I was told by another Korean guard that, following the occupation of his country, the Japanese had murdered both his father and his mother and had forced his sister into prostitution in an army brothel. Whether or not this tale was true, I have no means of telling, but it is a historical fact that the colonisation of Korea by Japan was a brutal and ruthless process, and the effect of it was clearly discernible in the uneasy relationship which existed between the Koreans and the Japanese on the Burma Railway. All the Koreans with whom I came in contact were prison guards and none of them held rank above the level of lowest private. They were obsequious in the extreme towards their Japanese officers and clearly went in fear of them. Whenever one of these popinjays appeared, the Korean would leap to attention as if released by a coil spring, bow deeply and constantly, and race at breakneck speed to carry out whatever orders might be given. This abject servility reacted unfortunately on the relationship between Korean guards and their prisoners. Being over anxious to please their masters, some of the Koreans treated us quite badly, believing (no doubt) that this was the kind of behaviour which the Japanese required of them. In other words, allowed to behave naturally, I think the Koreans on the whole would probably have treated us a good deal better than they often in fact did.

Soon after the Punch and Judy affair I saw another Korean humiliated by the Japanese, but in a more subtle fashion. He was a guard and he came on duty in the camp with a large sticking plaster over his mouth. The reason for the plaster was unclear but I assume it was a punishment. He performed the normal duties of a guard, marching back and forth with his rifle over his shoulder, but bereft of speech. We bowed to him as usual when our paths crossed, and he often as not responded with a nod and a grunt. Fortunately, we were not given to deep conversation with the guards, so the man's enforced silence was not a great problem, but I did wonder what might have happened if, owing to some sudden crisis, he had deemed it essential to speak. Would he have thrown caution to the wind, ripped off the plaster and given voice or would he, in his frustration have resorted to violence? There was no telling but I thought it wise to avoid him as far as possible. On the day after this bizarre episode the same guard was on duty again in the camp, his plaster removed.

I quite liked the garden work. It entailed no great effort; it was a healthy open air activity (except when it rained) and it brought in a small amount of much needed money, but the plum job at Tamarkan was the Hill Party. This consisted of about a dozen prisoners who were taken daily to the gun site. They spent the morning chiefly working in and about the Japanese cookhouse, were given a generous midday meal from Japanese rations and, in the afternoon, were required to carry rations up a nearby hill where a group of Japanese infantry manned a machine gun near the summit. The ration carrying was hard work but was rewarded with double rations at the evening meal when the party returned to the camp. Assignment to the Hill Party thus generated two extra large meals in one day. Small wonder therefore that it was extremely popular. In fact it was so popular that, as with the Town Party at Tavoy some two years earlier, selection had to be strictly regulated by roster.

After a long wait, my day on the Hill Party eventually arrived and off we went to the gun site. The first part of the morning was spent peeling and preparing vegetables in the kitchen. For the rest of the morning we were employed on emptying, cleaning and repacking a water filter. The filter was a large wooden box containing rounded stones in a graduated formation with the largest at the top. At midday we were given a thick stew with good quality rice, and in the afternoon we set off up the hill with the rations for the machine gunners. We went in pairs, each pair with a bamboo pole from shoulder to shoulder and the rations, packed in baskets, slung beneath. The path up the hill was steep and long. but the guard who was with us allowed us frequent rests and we were not therefore unduly exhausted when we reached the machine gun post towards the top.

The panoramic view of the prison camp, the bridges and the antiaircraft gun site was splendid, but I was concerned about the purpose of the machine gun. It appeared that it had been installed as a backup to the antiaircraft guns, but there was clear risk that shots from the machine gun might well hit prisoners in the camp, especially in the heat of battle, and I made a mental note to keep my head well down if either the bridges or the gun site happened to be attacked. When we returned to the prison camp we received, as promised, our double ration at the evening meal. The meal that night happened to include a doover, so we got two of those as well, which was an unexpected bonus. It was rare as a prisoner of the Japanese, to feel fully satisfied at the end of any meal, but at the end of this one I was more than satisfied. I felt bloated and I enjoyed the unfamiliar experience.

My gardening phase at Tamarkan was brought to an abrupt end by an attack of malaria. The attack surprised me because I had always observed preventative measures which, hitherto, had seemed effective. The preventive measures consisted of sleeping at night with my blanket completely covering me, including my head, and training myself to sleep motionless on my back to avoid the risk of uncovering myself and letting in the dreaded mosquito. Some may feel that such precautions were of doubtful value but it is a fact that in the jungle camps, where the disease was rife, I did not succumb to it. Perhaps on reaching the safer environment of the Thailand plain I unconsciously relaxed my strict regime, or perhaps my blanket (threadbare from the start) finally developed interstices large enough to admit the infectious insect. Whatever the cause, the effect was clear enough: recurrent rigor, high temperature and sweating. I obtained quinine from the medical officer but could not work for two or three weeks. I also had the misfortune at this time to fall down a monsoon drain. These were trenches about a yard deep which we dug round each hut to absorb the heavy rain. It was night; it was raining and I had to go to the latrine. At the entrance to the hut, the monsoon drain was crossed by a narrow bridge of planks. Being dizzy from the effects of the malaria, I missed my footing on the bridge and fell into the drain....striking the right side of my chest on the edge of the parapet. The fall caused considerable pain and was an added annoyance which I could have well done without while suffering from malaria. The medical officer said I had probably cracked a rib but assured me that, in any case, the pain would gradually disappear. It did, but it persisted long after I had recovered from the malaria.

When I recovered from the malaria I was given a new job on the duck farm. There were about two hundred full-grown ducks and three hundred and fifty ducklings. I was assigned to the ducklings department. Young ducks are normally endearing little creatures covered in soft yellow down, but those at Tamarkan were bald and scrawny. There were apparently two reasons for this. Firstly, I think the climate was against them, especially the rain, from which they had no shelter, and secondly their inadequate diet, which consisted of scraps from the prisoners' kitchen. They were a hideous sight and always seemed hungry. If any of us happened to have an uncovered ulcer on the leg (as many of us did) the ducklings would peck it.

Every morning we had to count the ducklings. This was done by herding the creatures from one bamboo enclosure to another, through a narrow gap. It was difficult to prevent more than one bird at a time from passing through the gap and we consequently often miscounted. When this happened. which was frequently, the Korean guard who was in charge of us (a man we nicknamed "Buffhead") would make us go through the whole process again. The morning count was thus an extremely exhausting process, not least for the ducks. But rain at night was our biggest bugbear. When this occurred there were always heavy casualties among the ducklings and our job, at the crack of dawn, was to resuscitate as many as possible. Having lit a fire, we would gather up the ducklings which were lying inert in the mud and range them round the blaze. The warmth would revive some of them but many would be beyond aid and would be laid out in neat rows to be taken into account at the subsequent "tenko". Buffhead would eventually arrive, and the more dead ducklings there were the more angry he was. It was therefore wise, on such occasions, to keep oneself as far as possible beyond striking distance. The count would take place as usual and the resulting fluttering and struggling would cause several of the recently revived birds finally to give up the ghost, thus adding further to the death role and to the increasing anger of Buffhead. This "morning after" pantomime occurred several times during my short period on the duck farm, and severely depleted our flock.

After a month or so of working with the ducklings, those of us in charge of them were suddenly dismissed. At the same time, the prisoners in charge of the pigs (a separate department) were also given the sack The trigger for the dismissals appears to have been the sudden and mysterious death of one of the pigs, though precisely how the pigs and the ducks became connected in the Japanese mind is not entirely clear. The constant depletion of the duckling flock was probably a factor, but when the axe fell it was nevertheless a considerable surprise.

One of the men appointed to replace the dismissed duck handlers was my friend, Stan Vaisey. Stan was full of confidence that improvements could be wrought.

"All you need," he said, "is a decent shelter and some green stuff in their diet."

"How are you going to fix that?" I asked.

"We can rig up some shelter with bamboo," he replied, "and, if we can't get anything better, we can give them grass to eat." I thought his proposals somewhat vague, but I was in no mood to dispute with him.

I wasn't greatly sorry to say goodbye to the ducks. The wretched environment in which they struggled for survival was of no special attraction to me. what did perturb me was the information, received shortly after leaving the duckery, that I had again been posted up country. This prospect filled me with apprehension for, in addition to the obvious danger of jungle life the hard labour and the disease there was now the added risk of being bombed by our own aircraft which, if rumour was correct, were becoming increasingly active along the length of the Railway. I had now been a prisoner for two and a half years. I had survived the construction of the Railway in Burma and a further spell on the Railway at Indato. I had begun to think that such expeditions were a thing of the past, but here I was on my way up country again and I was nonplussed, to say the least.

It was late afternoon when we assembled, in intermittent drizzle, at the side of the Railway, outside Tamarkan camp. We were a bedraggled band. As usual, we had a long wait for the train. It was dark when it arrived, and we were soaked. I had been expecting box cars, but the train consisted entirely of open wagons. We climbed up and settled ourselves on the wet floorboards, among the various packages and objects which were already aboard. The engine whistled and the train lurched forward in a series of jerks which caused a great clanging of the buffers. I tried to sleep but I was continually awakened by sparks from the wood-fired engine landing on my bare torso. In the end I gave up trying to sleep. I simply sat there, dabbing the sparks which regularly landed on my exposed flesh, and I smoked, which was a comfort.

We travelled all night, without stop, and when we halted at dawn it was in the midst of the jungle. We did not at first realise that we had reached our destination and we all sat tight. Then the guards got down and, with unmistakable shouts and gesticulations, made it clear that we also were required to detrain. We did so and the train left. We were paraded in three ranks along the narrow railway track and counted. We were then led through the trees to a muddy road; which in turn brought us to a small clearing. Here, tents were produced and we were told to erect them. Hitherto, we had regarded bamboo huts as a none too satisfactory form of shelter, but sight of the tents caused many of us to revise that opinion, especially when we discovered that several of the tents had holes in them. One tent was particularly badly torn and this caused ructions among its occupants, all anxious to secure bedspaces farthest from the gashes in the canvass. In adversity the British traditionally pull together, except perhaps in real life.

Having been fed at midday, on the customary rice and watery stew, we were paraded and marched off along the muddy road again, until we came to a spot where several piles of logs had been collected. Our job was to corduroy the road with these logs. I had not previously heard the word "corduroy" applied in this sense, but there were clearly some amongst us who had, and the word quickly became common parlance. In this process the logs are laid transversely across the road and their ends are bound together with wire. It didn't seem to me that a road surfaced in this manner would be likely to stand up to much traffic, especially in the hollows where the mud was at its thickest, but it intrigued me that the Japanese had had to resort to such a measure. Clearly the Railway was not proving as reliable as had been hoped, presumably because it was being regularly damaged by air attack. This was certainly my hope, though with the reservation that I wished to be well clear of the target area in the event of any such attack.

My first few days at the work site were spent carrying the logs from the several heaps and positioning them across the road. It was miserable work. The logs were muddy and wet and it was difficult, with bare feet, to keep one's balance on the slippery ground. Later. I did some felling and trimming of logs, which was an equally unattractive occupation. A lorry was provided for transporting the logs, but it all too frequently became stuck in the mud and had to be unloaded, hauled to drier ground and then reloaded. The whole process was primitive in the extreme and seemed to me to be doomed to failure. I had, of course, no particular wish to be involved in Japanese projects which were a success, but nor did I wish to be involved in useless schemes which rendered me vulnerable and miserable. I had a strong feeling that the war, at this stage, was moving in our favour. My hope of survival was therefore in the ascendant and the last thing I wanted was needless exposure on hopeless projects.

After a week or two of dispiriting labour with the logs, I suddenly fell victim to a sharp attack of the squits. "Squits" is a slang expression which was widely used on the Railway to cover all degrees of looseness of the bowel from a "touch of the trots" (another useful piece of slang) to full blown dysentery. The word apparently is a combination of "squirt" and "shit" which, ignoring the blatant vulgarity, is quite a subtle piece of etymology.

The squits assailed me one morning, shortly after arrival at the work site. I consequently spent a miserable day constantly repairing to the bush and, in between, trying to appear useful on a job which hourly grew more irksome. I was also mindful of my experience at Mergui, where dysentery had almost finished me, and when I returned to camp in the evening I lost no time in reporting sick. I was excused work, which was a step in the right direction, but no treatment was available and I spent a worrying week without much sign of improvement. Then, when I did begin to recover, and had already started to think in terms of soon having to return to work, I was unexpectedly told by the medical officer that I had been put on a list of men to be sent back to Tamarkan. I naturally did not question this decision but I have to say I was most agreeably surprised.

Early next morning I was happily ensconced in a box wagon with two other prisoners and a guard travelling south. The other prisoners were a Dutchman with suspected appendicitis and an American with undiagnosed abdominal pain. They both looked very seedy and, by comparison, I felt quite a fraud.

At about midday we stopped at Wampo, which is thirty-seven miles north of Tamarkan. Here a British prisoner, employed as a motor mechanic, brought us rice and a generous ladle each of kachangiju, which is dried peas (cooked). It was a good meal compared with our normal fare, but the Dutchman and the American, having no appetite, ate very little. I, on the other hand, was very hungry and tucked into my ration with gusto. Seeing this, the Japanese guard said to me:

"You! You no beeokee!"

The challenge took me by surprise and the first thought that flashed through my mind was "Oh God, he's going to have me sent back up the line". Then, upon reflection, I thought this seemed unlikely, but I felt it necessary to put forward some sort of defence, so I said:

"Today OK. Yesterday beeokee. Tomorrow maybe beeokee again."

It sounded a bit lame and the guard did 't look at all convinced, so I slowed down my rate of eating and left some of the rice, with reluctance. I was far from satisfied that these manoeuvres made much impression either, but I couldn't think of anything more to do or say.

174

The guard did not pursue his accusation and this led me to think he had perhaps been simply joking. I certainly hoped so. although I had never regarded the Japanese as much given to humour.

We trundled onward and were nearing the end of our journey when the guard suddenly announced:

"We go Chungkai."

"No," we chorused, "Tamarkan."

"Chungkai", said the guard firmly.

"Why Chungkai?" queried the American.

"Chungkai birry good camp," replied the guard.

"No," said the American, "Tamarkan number one."

"Chungkai number one," insisted the guard. "Tamarkan number ten."

Surely, I thought, the guard would have no discretion in such a matter. He would have his instructions as to point of delivery and would not dare to depart from them. It then occurred to me that perhaps his instructions were to deliver us to Chungkai. We had nothing against this camp; in fact it had a good reputation, but we were familiar with Tamarkan and had friends there. No more was said on the subject and in half an hour we reached Chungkai. But the train did not stop. It went on, across the steel bridge, and deposited us at Tamarkan. I knew then that our guard was a joker, which was a considerable relief, especially in relation to the "no beeokee" episode, which I was certain now would be pursued no further.

Chapter Eleven - Friendly Fire at Kwai Bridge

I was considerably relieved to be back at Tamarkan. I felt, in a sense, that I was returning home, especially as I found myself housed in the same hut as I had occupied prior to leaving for the tented camp. Very little had changed. One or two friends had disappeared, including Stan Vaisey, who had been posted up country, and a somewhat peculiar night guarding system had been introduced, but otherwise conditions were much as when I had left. Concert parties were still a regular feature of camp life and prisoners continued to vie for inclusion in the ever popular Hill Party.

Under the night guarding system, a prisoner had to stand guard at the entrance to every hut. Each guard's tour of duty was two hours and at the end of his stint he had to wake the next man on the roster before retiring to bed. Also at the entrance to each hut. there were two bamboo cups. One of these had ten slivers of bamboo in it and when a prisoner went out of the hut to the latrine, he had to transfer one of the bamboo slivers to the empty cup. On returning. he had to put back his sliver in the first cup. At irregular intervals the Korean guard would appear and put a question in Japanese. I cannot remember the words but the required reply if there was nothing to report, was "Eeju arrimassen". If a man was at the latrine the required reply was "one man benjo" and the Korean could then, if he wished, check that the corresponding sliver had been transferred to the empty cup. If it had ultimately been discovered that a prisoner, instead of going to the latrine, had escaped, then I presume the guard on the hut would have been held responsible. The essence of the system, apparently. was that risk of bringing retribution on a comrade would deter any would-be escapee. The concept was quite subtle but what fascinated me was why the Japanese had suddenly become so escape conscious. No one had tried to escape since the early days of our captivity, so why the present concern? My conclusion was that the answer lay in the progress of the war. The Japanese were beginning to experience reverses and they felt that if prisoners got wind of the fact their interest in escape might well be rekindled.

On the morning after returning to Tamarkan, I reported to the medical officer and he put me on the sick list for three days. He then put me on light duty (which attracted half pay) and I was allocated to the butchering party, whose daily job was to kill and dress a bullock for the prison kitchen. The butchers were Australian prisoners, four of them, and they were assisted by two light duty men whose main function was to help carry the meat from the slaughter ground to the kitchen. The first operation of the butchering process was to separate the chosen beast from the small herd which was kept at the edge of the camp, put a halter on it and get it to the slaughtering site. This was on the side of the camp remote from the point where the herd was kept and a hundred yards or so beyond the camp perimeter. We therefore had a considerable distance to take the animal and if, as frequently happened, the bullock proved reluctant, we had quite a struggle, the halter man pulling at the front and the rest of us pushing from behind. Often the animal would lie down, but the Australians had a procedure for dealing with this. One of them would pour some water from his army canteen into the bullock's ear. This invariably brought the beast rapidly to its feet.

At the slaughter ground stood a scaffold and a rough hewn table. The scaffold consisted of a pair of tall timber uprights, set about six feet apart, with a crosspiece at their top. In the ground beneath this structure a sizeable hole had been dug. On arrival here, the animal's head would first be tightly secured with the halter low down on one of the upright timbers of the scaffold. One of the butchers would then stun the bullock with a heavy hammer blow to the forehead. Next one end of a rope, which had been slung over the crosspiece of the scaffold, would be tied to the animal's hind legs and the beast would be hauled to a vertical position. Its throat would then be cut, the blood running conveniently into the hole in the ground beneath the animal's head. The carcass would then be skinned, dressed and quartered, and the residues thrown in the hole. Throughout this process increasing numbers of vultures would arrive and perch in the surrounding trees, ready to pounce on the rejected offal as soon as we vacated the site. They were grisly looking creatures, with scrawny necks and outsize black wings, but they performed the valuable task of keeping the site completely clean.

For purposes of carrying the meat back to the camp, the working party was split into three pairs, each pair carrying a portion of the meat slung from a bamboo pole, but I and my light duty partner seemed always to be allocated the largest portion. However, as the carrying was the only real work we were called upon to do we were hardly in a position to complain. It was, nevertheless, a back breaking job, especially as we could not pause for rest. This was partly because, if we had laid down the load, we would probably never have been able to pick it up again, and partly because we didn't want to contaminate the meat with dirt from the road. The daily five minute journey back to camp was thus a considerable struggle and I was never so glad as when we reached the kitchen and were able to dump our load.

Having watched the butchering process on the first day at the slaughter ground and found my presence unnecessary, I subsequently absented myself while the killing was being performed. This practice had a beneficial result: I discovered a group of lime trees with fruit on them. I gathered some of the limes, took them back to camp and sold them to the canteen. The price paid was pretty miserable but by repeating the procedure on a daily basis I managed to raise a small amount of much needed cash. A few limes I also consumed myself. I was not particularly fond of them, because they were sour and I had no sugar to put on them but they were a source of vitamin 'C'.

After a week or so of light duty with the slaughtermen I was pronounced fit again, and was waiting to be allocated to a full-time job when, late one afternoon, a group of about a dozen officer prisoners was marched into the camp. As I casually surveyed them I suddenly became aware that Flying Officer Smith, who had been the officer in charge of the radar station on Singapore Island, was among them. He and I had been on particularly cordial terms, partly as a result of his naturally informal manner (he belonged to the Royal Canadian Air Force) and partly as a result of our common interest in amateur radio. We were thus delighted to see one another again and we spent a long time exchanging experiences of the two and a half years which had elapsed since our parting at Padang. As our conversation proceeded it suddenly occurred to me that here was an opportunity to borrow some cash. At first, I dismissed the idea as unworthy. It would be taking advantage of our friendship, and might even destroy it. But the idea kept recurring, and in the end I convinced myself that no harm would result. I therefore popped the question, but I got a surprisingly disappointing reply. He had been playing poker, had lost heavily, and was consequently broke. It was, of course, no business of mine as to how F/O Smith disposed of his income, but I have to say that his profligacy astonished me.

Having failed to secure a loan, I turned my attention to an alternative possibility-that of obtaining a batman's job. Could F/O Smith do anything for me in this area? The Japanese (at Tamarkan) allowed one batman for every six officer prisoners, and as a dozen or more officers had recently arrived, it seemed that at least two such posts were available. F/O Smith said he would investigate and let me know, but when I went to see him the next day he told me there was doubt about my suitability because of my recent attack of dysentery. I said I hadn't had dysentery; I'd simply had a touch of the trots and that the MO would no doubt confirm this. I was sure he would, but I wasn't so sure that he would be prepared to declare me positively free from infection, which was what I knew the officers wanted, especially in relation to the handling of food. A day or two passed and eventually, one morning, F/O Smith hailed me on the parade ground. I braced myself for the worst, but he told me the job was mine. I was to serve six of the newly arrived officers, including F/O Smith. I was delighted.

A batman at Tamarkan didn't have a great deal to do. He fetched the officers' meals three times a day from the cookhouse, served them and did the washing up afterwards. Each morning he also swept the dirt floor of his officers' quarters, but otherwise the day was his own. He was paid for performing these extremely light duties and he was excused from both the morning and the evening tenkos. In short, the job was a "doddle".

Shortly after securing the batman's post I happened one day, to be chatting to Leading Seaman Bone who was employed in the Japanese cookhouse. He told me he had access to Japanese officers' toilet paper and asked me if I wanted any. This material, though not widely available, was ideal for rolling cigarettes. I therefore decided to buy a small quantity, add a modest profit and offer it to our officers. The response on the first day was moderate, the officers obviously not being familiar with the quality of the product but as more of them tried it and knowledge of it spread, so the sales increased until, very soon, demand exceeded supply. Boney would bring me a quantity each evening and I would sell the whole of it the next morning at breakfast time. I asked him to increase the supply but there were limits to the amount which he could safely purloin and I was therefore never able fully to meet the demand. When this became apparent, some of the officers-those determined not to be disappointed-began to buttonhole me each morning at first light as I crossed the parade ground which lay between my quarters and the officers'. This practice I thought somewhat unfair but, being in no position to regulate the behaviour of the officers, all I could do was to ration those who demanded unreasonably large quantities. This ensured at least a limited supply for those officers who were waiting in their quarters to buy in the normal manner. If I could have secured increased supplies, I could have expanded the venture to embrace a much wider field of customers. As it was, I could never get enough paper even to satisfy the officers. Profits were therefore limited but were sufficient to enable me for several weeks to buy from the canteen such items as eggs, bananas, peanuts, etc which normally would have been quite beyond my pocket. It was, therefore, as we would nowadays say, a "nice little earner".

The year 1944 was now drawing to a close and my mood was optimistic. Camp conditions generally were tolerable and my personal circumstances were the best I had so far experienced as a prisoner. My spirits were also buoyed up by constant rumour of Allied successes. We in the ranks still had no hard news but many of the rumours were so persistent that I became convinced of their truth. It thus seemed that at last the war was coming to an end and that if one could keep going for just a little longer there was good chance of survival. But war is full of shocks and in November my optimism was heavily dented by a traumatic event which brought me uncomfortably close to sudden death. This was the Allied bombing of the nearby Japanese gun site. It happened one evening during tenko.

I was lying on my bunk, excused the tenko by virtue of my batman's job, when I suddenly became aware of the sound of approaching aircraft. There were only a few of us in the hut, perhaps a dozen, and at first none of us was unduly perturbed, but as the sound of the engines continued to increase, two or three of our number got up and went outside to reconnoitre. Tension mounted as we awaited their report, the noise of the engines ominously growing. Then one of the men outside shouted "There's a shower of them and they're coming straight for us!" We in the hut leapt to our feet and made a bolt for the trenches. As I went out of the hut I glanced momentarily upwards and saw the bombers, a huge number, in tight formation and almost upon us. They were on a flight path which would bring them first over the gun site and then over the camp. I jumped into the monsoon trench alongside the hut and lay flat in the bottom of it. The relentless throb of the engines grew rapidly louder. There was a burst of machine gun fire which came either from one of the aircraft or from the machine gun post on the hill and, immediately afterwards, I heard the awful swish of the falling bombs. Then came the explosions, a rapid ear splitting crescendo which shook the earth so violently that I felt I was disintegrating. Then suddenly silence again, except for the diminishing sound of the aircraft engines. I stood up on legs which had turned to jelly. There was a choking smell of cordite, and so much dust in the air that I could hardly see. Debris from the huts was lying everywhere and bits of atap were gently floating to the ground. As I scrambled out of the trench I noticed a foot length of railway line, balanced on the parapet. I was congratulating myself on not having been struck by this lethal fragment when suddenly a panic stricken voice from the darkness shouted "They're coming back!" This caused a stampede. Everyone who was able began to run madly across the camp towards the side remote from the gun site. As we approached the parade ground in the middle of the camp we were confronted by a lone Korean guard who, judging from his determined stance and the menacing position in which he held his rifle, seemed bent on halting us. But we were not to be stopped and when we came within a few yards of him, still running full pelt, he suddenly about faced and led the charge. On reaching the camp perimeter, which was marked by a post and wire fence, we went through it and into the banana plantation beyond it. Here we halted, some four hundred yards from our starting point, panting for breath, listening, and scanning the sky.

The aircraft did not return and, as darkness fell, the guard who had led the exodus, shepherded us gently back to the camp. He appeared subdued, perhaps feeling that his conduct had not been entirely in keeping with the gallant tradition of the Imperial Japanese Army.

There were varying opinions as to how many aircraft had been involved in the attack but the figure most commonly quoted was twenty-one. This, I therefore assumed, was close to correct. All four of the anti-aircraft guns had been put out of action and heavy casualties had been inflicted on the Japanese gunners, but one of the bombs had overshot the target and landed in the prison camp, demolishing three or four of the huts, killing eighteen prisoners and injuring many more. I was amazed at the size of the bomb crater in the camp. It was big enough to accommodate a double-decker bus.

A Korean guard had also been killed in the raid. He had been patrolling the fence nearest the gun site and nothing of him, apart from his battered steel helmet, had been found.

The men on the Hill Party had escaped unscathed. On the approach of aircraft they had been told to scatter and none of them had suffered injury. A Dutch member of the party, however, had had his water bottle (carried on a belt at the hip) penetrated by a machine gun bullet.

So far as I am aware, the British Battalion suffered only one casualty in the raid. This was Ted Finel, a London dustman who belonged to the Royal Artillery. On being dug from the wreckage he was found to have, among other injuries, a complicated fracture of the jaw. Under treatment at the camp hospital, including some expert wiring of the broken jaw, he gradually recovered. Matelot Wright also had to be dug out but, miraculously, was unharmed.

The raid on the Tamarkan gun site was no more than a minor incident in the Far Eastern War but I had never previously witnessed such a decisive strike against the Japanese and it impressed me greatly. It was first hand evidence of the increasing power of the Allies and it convinced me that we would eventually win the. war. But the success of the raid was overshadowed by the deaths of eighteen fellow prisoners, men who had survived upwards of two and a half years of extreme maltreatment at the hands of the Japanese. only to be wiped out in an instant by their own forces. The only slight comfort was that the attack had taken place during tenko when the huts had been almost empty. If it had occurred at any other time the huts would have had far more men in them and the casualty level might well have been multiplied by as much as ten. This was a chilling thought, and not only in relation to the recent tragedy, for it was fully expected that the bombers would shortly return, next time to attack the bridges.

Fear of a raid on the bridges had an unsettling effect on the prisoners, especially those of us who were still housed at the vulnerable end of the camp. Whenever aircraft were heard, even at a distance, and whether by day or by night, there was invariably a rush for the trenches. Night-time panics were the worst. Often I would suddenly be wakened by what sounded like a crescendo of rapid rifle shots. The noise in fact came from loosely laid bamboo slats which formed our sleeping platform. These rattled violently as men hurriedly trampled across them in the race for the trenches and to me, in my first few moments of half consciousness, the clatter sounded like a fusillade. I never thought there was any great risk of night attack, but panic is contagious, and whenever a nocturnal exodus occurred I always joined it.

During daylight, on several occasions, single aircraft flew close to and over the camp. We watched these machines warily from our trenches as they cruised about, largely unopposed. Antiaircraft guns at times fired on them, but not in any concentrated fashion. The machine gun on the hill also let off an occasional burst but was eventually silenced by a bomber whose crew apparently became exasperated. The plane which decided to retaliate first circled in a wide arc which brought it facing the hill. It then flew directly at the machine gun post, firing as it went. What damage was inflicted we could not tell but we heard no more from the machine gun, which we felt was a hopeful sign.

On one daylight occasion, at about noon, we heard the familiar sound of aircraft engines and, as usual, took to the trenches. When the planes came into view, high in the sky, we were amazed at their number. There were scores of them and we braced ourselves for the inevitable attack on the bridges which we had been expecting. On came the planes, the rhythmic throbbing of their engines growing louder by the second. We crouched lower in the trenches, expecting the bombs to be released at any moment, but the menacing beat of the engines began to recede and we gradually realised to our great relief that the armada had passed over us. Then, before the noise had completely died away, there came a second wave of aircraft from the same direction. They also passed harmlessly overhead and were followed by more and more aircraft in what seemed an unending procession. The display must have lasted a full twenty minutes and our spirits rose as each new wave of aircraft made its appearance. How many aircraft there were in all I hesitate to guess, but there were certainly hundreds. Their target also remains a mystery, but they were heading approximately northward which would have been in the direction of Burma.

It was late one afternoon when the bridges were eventually bombed. A single aircraft appeared and began to overfly the camp and its surroundings. It was fairly high and did not seem to us particularly belligerent, but we took to the trenches nevertheless. For two or three minutes the plane continued to patrol unmolested, sometimes directly above us, sometimes out of sight. Then a distant battery of anti-aircraft guns opened up and we saw shells begin to explode around the plane. Some of the shells appeared quite close to the aircraft but it continued on its course, apparently undamaged. Then the gunners sent up another salvo, and as we watched the further burst of shells a second aircraft suddenly roared like lightning diagonally across the camp at tree top height. It materialised and was gone again in seconds but it was so low that I glimpsed the face of one of its crew. I also recall seeing the detailed camouflage markings on the side of the aircraft as it sped like a rocket across my field of vision. Then, as the roar of the plane engines died swiftly away, there was a series of massive explosions from the direction of the bridges. We were not certain at this stage that the bridges had been hit but we let forth an anticipatory cheer, accompanied by a barrage of joyful expletives to express our admiration of the cunningly designed attack which we had just witnessed. We rejoiced, I might add, not only at the skill of the raid but also that none of our lives had been sacrificed in the process.

When the raid was over, the Japanese called for a tenko on the parade ground, of all prisoners without exception. We obliged them and, as we were being counted in the growing darkness, we noticed a glow in the southern sky. This grew rapidly bigger, in stages marked by sudden increases of illumination. It was obviously a major conflagration which was out of control. As it spread across the horizon, growing wider and higher by the minute, word came that it was the petrol storage tanks at Nong Pladuk which had been bombed and set on fire. It was an impressive spectacle; huge light, majestic and soundless, intermittently erupting like a volcano. Nong Pladuk was the point where the Burma Railway branched off from the main Bangkok to Singapore Line. Here the Japanese had army workshops, ammunition dumps and petrol stores. Nong Pladuk was a good thirty miles from Tamarkan but the brilliance of the fires made it seem much closer.

During the tenko we also learned that both the bridges had been hit, the steel bridge losing three complete spans close to its centre. We were overjoyed, and the Japanese were downcast and surly.

At Nong Pladuk, in addition to the military establishments, there was also a prisoner of war camp. Miraculously, none of the prisoners there was injured on the occasion of the bombing of the petrol dump but, shortly afterwards, during a night raid on an ammunition train which prisoners were loading, eighty of the Nong Pladuk prisoners were killed. Ironically, the prisoners loading the train were not the victims. They were given sufficient warning to enable them to reach safety. It

185

was prisoners asleep in the camp who were killed, by a single stray bomb. Reports of such carnage were extremely disturbing. We knew that the end of the war was near, but increasing danger from our own bombers made us begin to wonder if we would survive to see it.

The steel bridge at Tamarkan remained unrepaired and unusable for the rest of the war but the Japanese, aided by a sizeable working party of prisoners from the camp, began repairing the wooden bridge on the day after the raid. I was not involved in this operation but I had friends who were, and they did not relish the job. This was partly because much of the work was in the middle of the bridge, thus making a quick getaway difficult in the event of an air raid and partly because, on the river bank, there were several unexploded bombs which the Japanese did not deal with until some time after work on the bridge had begun. The bombs meanwhile were simply marked with red flags.

A day or two after work on the wooden bridge began, I was detailed to join a party of prisoners destined for Chungkai camp, a mile or so from Tamarkan on the other side of the river. We crossed the river by means of a wide pontoon bridge built by Japanese army engineers and arrived at the new camp about noon. The midday meal •was served and we were then told, somewhat to our surprise, that we were required for a working party that night. We duly assembled at dusk, after eating our evening meal, and were then marched back across the bridge. On the northern bank of the river we saw a stationary train loaded with Japanese soldiers and military equipment, and on the southern bank there was a second train, also stationary, made up entirely of closed box wagons. It was now dark but the area around the second train was illuminated by a huge bonfire.

The doors of the box wagons were unlocked and thrown open to reveal stacks of dark green boxes. These we were told to unload and pile beside the track. We went to work and very quickly the anti-aircraft gunners among us identified the freight as 4.5 inch British Army anti-aircraft shells, packed two per box. The boxes were of steel and one of them, plus its contents, was as much as two of us could lift. It took about three hours to unload the ammunition and throughout this period I kept thinking what a foolish idea it was to have lit the bonfire. Word could quite easily have been passed to the Allies that an ammunition train was available for attack (as presumably had happened at Nong Pladuk) and the bonfire would have made a perfect marker. With these thoughts in mind, I began to feel that the wooden bridge, despite the mid-river perch, might well have been a safer job on which to be employed.

Having emptied the train, we then had to carry the ammunition, again two men per box, the three hundred yards or so across the pontoon bridge to the other side of the river, meeting on the way Japanese troops bringing field guns, mules and office equipment in the opposite direction. On reaching the far bank, we stowed the ammunition in the box cars of the train being emptied of field guns etc, and returned to the south bank carrying office furniture.

It was hard and (in my opinion) dangerous work and it took us all night to complete, but at dawn we were given a lift back to camp on the train returning northward to Burma. As our train moved off, we sitting in open trucks, the Japanese Officer in charge of operations stood at the side of the track solemnly bowing and saluting us. This presumably was intended as a gesture of thanks but, in the eyes of pressed men, it was nothing but hypocrisy, an art at which the Japanese are past masters.

We did this transhipment work every night for, I suppose, about a fortnight which, so far as I can remember, was the time it took to repair the wooden bridge and restore its track.

Owing to the language barrier, it was difficult to converse with the Japanese troops who nightly were brought back from the Burma front, but on several occasions I made a point of putting the question:

"Burma OK ga?"

The sort of reply I got was either:

"Birruma birry bad", or

"Birruma orroo bum-bum".

This latter comment would often be accompanied by a rapid raising and lowering of down facing palms to indicate heavy bombing. It was thus clear that, at least in Burma, the enemy was getting a heavy pasting. which cheered me considerably.

On the day following the completion of the repair of the wooden bridge, the Allies again bombed it and put it out of action. At Chungkai we heard the explosions but were too far away to see the event. News. however, that the bridge had once again been successfully attacked reached us very quickly. I was impressed not only by the success of the attack, but also by the fact that the Allies had timed their raid to correspond with the completion of the repair work. Espionage seemed to me the only possible explanation and this thought disturbed me in relation to the transhipment job. It now seemed more than likely that the Allies were aware of this operation. especially as it was a nightly event. And yet we had not been attacked, despite the regular bonfire. Fortunately, my worries on this score were quickly swept away by an announcement that no further night working parties would be required from the Chungkai force. The reason for this decision was a mystery. Perhaps in future the Japanese intended to use Tamarkan prisoners for the work, or perhaps the job was rendered impossible by damage to the pontoon bridge during the recent raid. I could not tell, but I never worked again at the Tamarkan bridges.

Chapter Twelve - Saved by the Atomic Bomb

After the night shifts at Tamarkan finished, I remained at Chungkai for another fortnight or so, during which I had no opportunity to work except on the occasional camp chore, which attracted no payment. Paid work, however, was no longer my first priority. I much preferred to be unemployed at Chungkai than to be gainfully employed at a dangerous place such as Tamarkan.

One of my first chores at Chungkai was sweet potato peeling in the camp kitchen. There I fell into conversation with a British Army prisoner who had been involved in the construction of the Railway from the Thailand end. We talked first about the various rumours which were going the rounds regarding the progress of the war and, in particular, about an alleged landing by American troops on the Philippine Islands. If this news was true (and we were inclined to think it was) then a direct attack on Japan itself, we thought, might well be imminent. All seemed to hinge on the distance between the two places and neither of us was certain on this, but we agreed that at least the war was now moving in the right direction.

Having exhausted the war news, we turned to more personal matters, my fellow spud peeler (I never knew his name) revealing that a month or two previously he had undergone a colostomy operation. This astonished me. I knew that medical facilities for prisoners had greatly improved since the completion of the Railway (largely. it was understood because the Japanese, becoming less confident of ultimate victory, had begun to allow improved supplies of medicines, etc, from the Red Cross) but I did not realise that prison hospitals had become well enough equipped to be able to carry out operations as sophisticated as a colostomy. In the case of my co-worker in the Chungkai kitchen, the operation had been performed at Nakhon Pathom, a prison hospital about forty miles west of Bangkok, which I had heard about but never seen. His hope now was that the war would end soon enough for him to have the operation successfully reversed. I wished him well but how he fared I do not know, since I never saw him again.

Tom Douglas, a lieutenant in the Royal Corps of Signals, was another interesting character I met at Chungkai, but never saw again. I came across him one evening whilst strolling round the camp. It transpired early in our conversation that we had a mutual interest in amateur radio and from then on our tongues never stopped wagging. I mentioned to him that I had a copy of the 1938 Radio Amateur's Handbook. This annual publication, produced by the American Radio Relay League, was, and still is, the technical bible of amateur radio enthusiasts world-wide. To me, as a prisoner, it represented happy times in the past and hope for the future. It was therefore precious and, during my years of captivity, I read it from cover to cover many times. All books, however, were subject to approval by the Japanese and mine had never been submitted because I knew full well that, with its copious illustrations of radio transmitters and receivers, it would never have been accorded the stamp of approval. Each time the Japanese had searched our possessions I had therefore had to conceal the book, and was concerned that eventually it would be discovered. Tom, surprisingly, said this was no problem. He would provide me with a forged stamp. This he did. It was a vertical label about half an inch wide and an inch and a half in length, bearing the appropriate Japanese characters, beautifully executed. I was slightly concerned on first displaying the book with its bogus label but with each successive inspection my confidence increased. It was a masterly deceit which worked admirably for the rest of my days as a prisoner. Tom, so far as I am aware, did not pursue his talent for forgery on being released. Instead he chose to become engineer-in-charge of the BBC television transmitter at Sutton Coldfield.

Another Chungkai inmate I have cause to remember was Leo Britt, a flamboyant character responsible for the management of the camp's theatre company. Britt had the air of a professional impresario and in civilian life may well have been one. During my brief sojourn at Chungkai I saw only one of his productions but it left a considerable impression on me. The play was Major Barbara by George Bernard Shaw whose works, prior to Chungkai, were completely unknown to me. This gap in my knowledge was the result of a grammar school curriculum devoid of the works of all living authors. Britt's Major Barbara was thus a revelation. I was intrigued with the plot of the play, especially its social aspects, and resolved to find out more about the author of it as soon as I could. This I have since done and the effort has been rewarding. But it was not the content alone of the play that fascinated me; it was also the quality of the production. Despite a daunting dearth of both materials and facilities, and a complete lack of female actors, Britt successfully presented a most ambitious piece in the most unpromising of circumstances.

I left Chungkai in January 1945, one of a group of about a hundred prisoners. We first marched the three or four miles to Kanburi and were then put on a goods train which took us to Ratchaburi, some twenty miles south of Nong Pladuk on the main Bangkok/Singapore line. Here we stayed a night in what appeared to be a public hall and on the following day were taken, again by train, a further thirty miles south to Phetburi.

The camp at Phetburi was of the standard pattern and stood at the foot of a hill on which there was a Buddhist temple. Yellow-robed priests from the temple, on their daily begging round among the local villagers, often passed through the camp as if they had an inalienable right to do so. Perhaps they owned the ground on which the camp was built; I could not tell but the Japanese, apart from preventing the priests from conversing with us, made no attempt to interfere with them.

Water for the camp kitchen at Phetburi had to be fetched daily from a pool near the temple and for this purpose we were provided with a lorry, some tubs and two or three ropes. The ropes were for hauling the lorry, which unfortunately had no petrol. It was hard work dragging the lorry, especially on the outward journey which was uphill, and there was a limit to the amount of water which we could transport by this primitive method. Drinking water in the camp was therefore rationed.

For purposes of bathing, we were taken each day to a marshy lily pond, inaccessible to the lorry, some four of five hundred yards outside the camp. From this pool, water could be taken back to the camp to augment the drinking water ration, but many did not possess the necessary containers and if they wanted extra drinking water they had to buy it from those who did. The practice of selling drinking water might, I suppose, be justified on the ground that work was involved in the supply of it. The water certainly had to be carried from the pool and boiled before being sold, but I thought it unethical to trade in such a vital necessity. Fortunately, with my minuscule can, capable of holding no more than a third of a pint. there was never any danger of my being tempted into this line of business.

Phetburi was a new and expanding camp when I arrived there. It did not therefore surprise me that my first regular job was hut building. This was congenial work which entailed nothing more than erecting a bamboo framework onto which we tied rectangular sections of atap to form the walls and roof. Later on we built an airstrip and also dug a huge bund round the camp.

The site of the airstrip was a mile or so from the camp. It had been cleared of trees and scrub by the time I started work there and my first job was stone breaking. I did not enjoy sitting in the broiling sun cracking rocks, especially as there was risk of splinters flying up and breaking my glasses. I should like to have had a pocket in which to stow the precious spectacles, but my g-string had no such facility. After some weeks of stone breaking we were next employed on carrying the broken stone in shovel shaped baskets onto the runway and spreading it. Each basket was carried by two prisoners one of whom, on reaching the dumping point was required to take the basket and spread its contents in a wide sweeping motion, the purpose of which was to achieve an even distribution. It was easy enough to do this but we were not in a co-operative mood and chose instead to dump the stone in heaps. This annoyed the guards who assumed we hadn't the ability to follow their instructions. They therefore kept taking hold of a basket of stones and demonstrating the technique. We made as if to try to understand and continued to dump the stone in heaps, which caused the anger of the guards to continue to rise. Macdougall was my stone spreading partner and the guard in charge of us was a tiny little man whom we nicknamed "Half Pint". Half Pint was not an unreasonable fellow but, having fruitlessly demonstrated the spreading technique on numerous occasions, he suddenly became exasperated and rushed at me as I dropped yet another basket of stones in a neat mound on the runway. I rapidly retreated striding backward with the basket held shieldlike in front of me. This caused general amusement particularly on the part of Macdougall who was grinning broadly as I went past him taking ever longer and more rapid backward steps. Then, when Half Pint reached Macdougall he suddenly halted, turned towards Mac and gave him an almighty slap in the face. Mac's grin was now replaced by a look of shock and injured innocence which for a moment or two deprived him of the power of speech. When he recovered, he said in a pained voice:

"Ah niver did a fuck' n thing"

This was true, but only in relation to the heap of stones which I had just dumped, Mac having earlier created some sizeable hummocks himself. The truth was that we were all culpable. Retribution was indicated and fell on the nearest prisoner available. I don't know why we chose so to provoke the Japanese on this particular day. Perhaps it was our growing confidence in the ultimate outcome of the war but it was a dangerous tactic and the slap suffered by Mac was a sharp reminder of the fact. It put an end to any further provocative behaviour on our part and we spent the rest of the day dutifully spreading the stone in the manner required.

Carrying and spreading the stone was not hard work but it was mindnumbingly dull and it went on for weeks. The only pleasurable event of our day was the walk from the camp to the airstrip through lightly wooded, sparsely populated. green countryside in the cool of the morning. At the airstrip the only noteworthy event was the daily appearance of a single aircraft, high in the sky. It was clearly a reconnaissance machine or, as Half Pint put it, a "come-see-go-back-speaku prane". It flew directly over us in a straight line, always at about eleven o'clock in the morning and, because of its great height, remained visible for several minutes. It was no danger to us but it crossed my mind that, as a result of its observations, our airstrip, when finished, might well eventually be attacked. This in fact never happened, the runway not being completed until the very end of the war. Ironically, however, the first aircraft to take off from it carried liberated prisoners to freedom from the nearby camp. I, however, by then, had moved on.

Before we left the airstrip job, Mac fell into further trouble, though not at the hands of the Japanese. During a midday break he and I discovered a mango tree a short distance from the runway. There was fruit on it and we decided to gather some. Mac would possibly say that I persuaded him to climb the tree but to the best of my recollection, he was a willing volunteer. It was a large tree and it took some time to reach the level where the fruit was growing, but Mac got there and began to throw down the mangoes for me to catch. All went well until he disturbed an ants' nest, the inhabitants of which immediately mounted a ferocious attack on him. For a while he battled gamely but, after a minute or two, he had to concede defeat and come down the tree. The ants were the giant sized red coloured variety and Mac was covered in them, especially on his legs, an area which, while clinging onto the tree, he had had particular difficulty in defending. On the ground I did my best to help him get rid of the ants but I was hampered by a prolonged bout of laughter which I found difficult to control. Although Mac, divested of the ants, seemed none the worse for his experience, the bites on his legs in fact festered and had to be treated by the MO. Mac consequently had reservations regarding the success of the operation. but it did result in a useful supply of green mangoes which, when ripe, we both enjoyed.

My last job at Phetburi was bund digging. The bund was a huge vertical sided ditch which completely encircled the camp. It was far too wide for a man to jump across and its depth was such that a man getting into it had no change of getting out again without the aid of a ladder. No previous camp had had a bund. Indeed in many camps the boundaries had not even been marked. We therefore naturally wondered why such a high degree of security was now considered necessary. The obvious answer was that the area in which the camp was situated was expected to become a battle zone where prisoners who broke free might well become a menace to the defenders. The prisoners therefore had to be more rigorously confined. This was the general opinion but some of us felt that the Japanese might well have a more sinister plan in mind, namely to liquidate us within the confines of the bund. This opinion was reinforced by the fact that, at Phetburi, the highest rank of prisoner was sergeant major, our commissioned officers having been separated from us. Fortunately the liquidation theory was never put to the test since there was no Allied landing in either Thailand or any of the surrounding countries. Instead, the war was brought to a dramatic and sudden end by the dropping of the atomic bombs on Hiroshima and Nagasaki. This act remains controversial but I have yet to meet an ex-prisoner of the Japanese who is prepared to condemn it.

The bunded camp at Phetburi seemed designed for final containment and I therefore expected to end the war there, either liberated or murdered by our treacherous enemy. It was consequently a surprise to find myself, in May 1945, once again on the move, this time to my twenty-fifth and final camp. Although I never actively enjoyed being constantly moved about by the Japanese, I think the frequent change of scene did much to obviate the boredom which would otherwise have been our lot, but I give no credit to the Japanese in this matter since they clearly shunted us from place to place for no purpose but their own.

The first leg of our journey was by goods train to Bangkok, a journey of about a hundred miles. We arrived in the middle of the night and were taken by barge to a godown on the side of the river. It was pitch black as we walked across the narrow plank which had been placed between the barge and the river bank and one of our number slipped and fell into the water. Frantic efforts were made to locate him and pull him out but he was never found. I did not know him but he was a Geordie and belonged to the Army. The rest of us were shepherded to the godown where we slept on a concrete floor for what remained of the night.

I didn't like Bangkok, particularly the dock area where we were housed. I imagined it as a place likely to be bombed by the Allies and I therefore regarded it as distinctly unsafe. Bombers did fly over us during our first night there and, although they attacked nothing in our vicinity, their presence did nothing to reassure me. It seemed likely that we would resume our journey the next day but in this I was disappointed. Instead, I found myself detailed to join a party of about a dozen men required for work at a nearby boat yard. As we marched along on our way to the yard I remember occasional distant glimpses of the strange architecture of Bangkok, especially the roofs of the buildings, ornately carved and curiously pinnacled. It was a city I would have much enjoyed exploring, though not in wartime as a prisoner of the Japanese.

The boat yard was on the waterfront a mile or so from the godown and we spent the day there carrying and stacking long lengths of planking. It was easy work and no pressure was put on us, but I thought it curious to have been given a job in the course of a journey from one camp to another. The craft in course of construction at the yard were all of the native type and the yard was obviously owned by Thais. It therefore seemed that we had been loaned for the day, no doubt at a price.

After a second night at the godown there was a rumour that during the night a Japanese guard, patrolling the quay, had been stabbed to death by Thais and flung into the river with a bamboo stake in his chest. Whether or not this was true I could not tell, but some of the prisoners said they had heard a scuffle and a scream in the early hours and this gave some credence to the story.

We spent a third night in the godown and then, at last, we resumed our journey, again by rail. The train on which we travelled consisted partly of carriages which had red crosses painted on their white roofs, and partly of box wagons. We were put in the box wagons. so it was clear that the red crosses were not intended as any protection for us, but who in fact travelled in the coaches I had no chance to see.

It was midday when we were put in the box wagons and the train did not depart until the evening. Meanwhile, the heat in the wagons, which were made of steel, became intense and the sweat rolled off us despite the fact that the doors of the wagons were left wide open. In addition to the discomfort of the heat, I continued to worry about the risk of air raid. A railway siding in the heart of the capital of Thailand seemed to me a prime military target which, sooner or later, was bound to be bombed. I therefore felt extremely apprehensive. Looking back over the years, I now think I was perhaps rather over anxious but the recent experiences at Tamarkan were still all too fresh in my memory.

We travelled from Bangkok first in an easterly direction. This was clear from the position of the setting sun, but in which direction we subsequently went it was impossible to say, owing to the darkness. We reached our destination in the early hours of the following morning. It was a country station which I now believe was probably Prachantakham, but I am still not certain. This place is some forty or fifty miles north-east of Bangkok. We detrained, were counted and led off along a red gravelled road.

At dawn, we halted for an hour or so, and were fed before resuming the march. At midday we halted again, this time in the welcome shade of some large trees on the outskirts of a village. Here we rested for about two hours and were fed on rice and stew. We then continued the march, which was on red gravel for the whole of our journey.

We reached our destination, Nakhon Nayok prison camp, at sunset and, despite the gravel roads, which were hard on bare feet, Mac and I finished the march in good shape. Many, however, suffered blistered feet, including one of the guards whose footwear was the standard rubber-soled bootee plimsoll with the separate cavity for the big toe. This type of footwear, incidentally, presented a cloven hoofed appearance which to my mind was always synonymous with the devil.

Some prisoners, through blistered feet and illnesses such as malaria, were unable to complete the march and were left at various places on the roadside. They were later picked up by lorry and brought to the camp. The length of the march was, I calculate, about twenty-five miles.

Nakhon Nayok was a large camp housing prisoners of British, Australian, Dutch and American nationality. It was built on flat paddy fields at the foot of a range of wooded hills which lay to the north of it, and it was in these hills that we were mainly employed by the Japanese.

It seemed to me that, in this hilly area, the Japanese were preparing a redoubt which they planned to defend in the event of Bangkok becoming untenable. Hidden under the trees there were numerous small petrol dumps. There were also extensive stables housing mules, a blacksmith's shop and several barrack huts. In the sides of the hills, field gun emplacements were being dug and in one of these a gun was already installed. I had my first sight of these defence works as a member of a working party delivering petrol to the site. The petrol, in forty gallon steel drums, we fetched by lorry from a railway station about an hour's journey from the camp. On reaching the hills, we stowed the drums in widely separated groups of about six, each group close under a tree. I was engaged in this work for several weeks and the number of drums transported must have been several hundred. I also spent a few days with a party detailed to dig one of the gun emplacements. This was hard work with little respite, unlike the petrol hauling job which had the benefit of long rides on the lorry. At the gun emplacement the Japanese soldier in charge of us, stripped to his g-string, at first joined us in the digging, but he was grossly overweight and, with sweat pouring off him, his pace became slower and slower until eventually he came to a permanent halt. Judging by his build he was probably a Sumo wrestler.

From the digging work we were transferred to hut building. The huts, it was said, were intended for the Japanese prisoner of war administration staff, who were to be evacuated from their Bangkok offices. This information reinforced my belief that the Japanese expected the Bangkok area shortly to become a battle zone, a prospect which I viewed with mixed feelings. It was exciting to think we might soon be released by the advancing Allies but at the same time I had misgivings regarding the treatment we might get if the Japanese became involved in a major retreat. This dilemma was dramatically resolved on 17 August 1945 when, at about eleven o'clock in the morning, a Japanese despatch rider on a motor cycle arrived at the building site. He had a brief conversation with the Japanese NCO in charge of the work, and rode off. The NCO then instructed us to stop work and fall in. We did so and were marched off in the direction of the camp. No one at this stage had told us that the war was over but one of the Korean guards who was marching with us said

"War finis. You me changey changey."

This seemed a clear enough statement that the war was at last over, but the suddenness of the event, and our fear of being disappointed. left some doubt in our minds. This was dispelled a few minutes later when we met a group of officer prisoners who were being marched in the opposite direction. They confirmed that the Japanese had indeed capitulated and this convinced us.

As we entered the camp, the guards sat motionless on their bench in front of the guardroom, making no attempt to count us as they normally did. They still had their rifles and they eyed us morosely. I had a fleeting thought that they might still molest us but my attention was swiftly diverted to the parade ground in the middle of the camp. Here on tall bamboo poles, flew the Union Jack, the Lion of Scotland, and the flags of Australia, USA and Holland, all proudly proclaiming that the Allies had won the war. It was a stirring moment which brought a huge lump to my throat. Then, some prisoners who were assembled on the parade ground began to sing "Oh God our Help in Ages Past". This destroyed the last vestiges of my self-control. I went to my hut, which was fortunately empty and wept for joy. I had never before experienced such emotion and was greatly embarrassed.

Later in the day we learned the cause of Japan's sudden surrender. It was the atomic bombs dropped on Hiroshima and Nagasaki. Such devices, we were led to believe, not only caused devastating explosions but also produced gamma rays which were even more lethal than the explosions. A Korean guard to whom I spoke referred to the bombings as "electric war". This expression, I imagine, was used generally by the Japanese and Koreans prior to becoming familiar with the term "atomic war". But what were these gamma rays, and why were they so deadly? Such questions we could not answer, but we were greatly impressed by the fact that it had taken only two of the new-fangled bombs to end the conflict and dramatically free us from three and a half years of miserable bondage. It didn't occur to any of us to have the slightest pity on the thousands of Japanese civilians killed by the bombs. This was partly because we didn't yet realise the enormity of an atomic bombing, and partly because we were filled with hate for the nation which had so grossly humiliated and maltreated us, and been responsible for the wretched deaths of so many of our comrades.

Although the Japanese surrendered on 15 August, they did not tell us that the war was over until two days later and I have occasionally wondered why this was so. Perhaps in an area as vast as the Far East there were communication difficulties, although in our situation at Nakhon Nayok, a mere fifty-five miles from Bangkok as the crow flies, this hardly seems likely. The alternative explanation is that it took some time for the Japanese to decide how to deal with the prisoners. There would certainly be some horror stories if the prisoners were merely released. Might it, therefore, not be more convenient to dispose of the prisoners to prevent such stories coming to light? These are questions which are unlikely to be answered, but it would be interesting to tabulate the dates on which the prisoners at the various camps were notified of the end of the conflict.

On the day after the Japanese admission that the war was over, a group of six or eight American soldiers walked into the camp. They had been dropped by parachute in the district some weeks earlier and had been involved in espionage activities. They were deep yellow in colour through constantly taking the anti-malarial drug mepacrine and they knew far more about the redoubt in the hills than we did. On the next day, two events occurred which made me feel that the war had positively ended. Firstly, the RAF flew over and dropped by parachute a supply of food and other necessities. Then a party of half a dozen British troops parachuted into the camp. I vividly recall my pleasure at talking with these rugged British parachutists, yet I recall not a single word that was said.

Much of the food which was dropped went into the camp cookhouse, but luxuries such as coffee, jam, bacon and cigarettes were issued to individuals. The bacon, which we fried for breakfast, was succulent.

A day or two after the dropping of the food we were given details of the plan for our evacuation. We were all to be taken by lorry to Bangkok airport. The Americans would leave first and be followed by the Australians, the British and The Dutch, in that order. The reason for the Dutch being bottom of the list was clear enough. The natives in the Dutch possessions such as Java and Sumatra were in armed revolt and travel arrangements were therefore difficult, but how the rest of the sequence had been arrived at we never knew. The British were certainly none too pleased at being ranked third in the queue, especially when it became known that it was going to take a fortnight to empty the camp.

It was tiresome to have to wait for our turn to be moved. We wanted to sleep in beds again, sit on chairs and eat food from a table, in short to be given our full liberty which, I must say, did not seem to me too much to ask, bearing in mind the length of our captivity. When Pitchon left with the American forces I gave him my home address and he undertook to let my family know that I had survived. This he did and the cablegram was duly received. I assumed that Pitchon and I would meet again at the collecting point in Bangkok but I, in fact, never saw him again.

Eventually our departure day arrived. On the previous evening we had been told to be ready to move at 9 am but we were packed and poised on the start line long before that time. Liberty at last was now in sight and we were eager to savour it. Then a messenger arrived to inform us that our departure had been postponed because the Countess Mountbatten had decided to visit the camp. This news was not well received, particularly by those of us, including myself. who were selected to build a latrine for the exclusive use of our distinguished guest. By local standards, the latrine which we constructed was luxurious. It had a wooden seat and was concealed in a bamboo and atap housing with a door. In due course the countess's cavalcade arrived, a string of half a dozen jeeps bearing an assortment of British and Japanese military dignitaries, in addition to the Countess herself. As the convoy entered the camp a modest cheer arose from those whose departure had not been interrupted and, from a standing position in her jeep, the Countess waved vigorously in response. She and her entourage then went into one of the huts apparently to be officially greeted and we, meanwhile, were instructed to gather on the parade ground. This we did and she shortly came out to address us. Among other things. she said she realised that, above everything else. we would want to have news of home. In this area, she told us, the most important recent event had been the General Election which had resulted in a new government.

It was a Labour Government "and a jolly good government too". Such a remark, from a person so clearly a member of the upper echelons of our Society, struck me as distinctly odd, but I later discovered that she was famous for her left wing political views which were a constant source of alarm to many of her upper class associates. At Nakhon Nayok, however, on the day she spoke to us, I was simply bewildered by what she said.

Having delivered her speech. the Countess did a walkabout among the inmates of the camp, chiefly asking questions. She wanted to know if we had enough food, whether we had cigarettes. etc. She mixed easily enough with the troops but I felt that they were somewhat inhibited by the Countess's gushing upper class diction. Having toured the camp, she withdrew again to the hut and remained there until late afternoon, when she and her convoy then left. I learned later that her visit to Nakhon Nayok had been part of a grand tour of Far Eastern prisoner of war camps, a private aeroplane having been specially provided for the purpose.

To wile away our time after the Countess completed her tour of the camp, Andy Macdougall, Harry Lander and I sat drinking locally made toddy which we had bought from a Thai. The toddy, a white coloured liquid, was contained in Mac's fire blackened tin can, which we passed from hand to hand. It was a pleasant drink which rapidly restored our customary cheerfulness. Indeed, having disposed of about three quarters of it, our mood became positively boisterous. I also experienced, however, some difficulty in concentrating my gaze and I decided that the time had come to call a halt. Mac was of the same opinion, but Harry continued to imbibe until the tin was empty. We were all sitting on the ground, Harry swaying slightly from the hips and occasionally putting a hand to the ground to preserve his balance. Harry's countenance was normally pale but it now turned a ghastly white. He continued to smile but his head developed an irregular wobble. To maintain his more or less upright position, he eventually put both his hands on the ground at a slight angle behind him, thus forming a tripodal support system. This would have been perfectly effective if one of his elbows had not suddenly buckled, thus causing him to collapse sideways in an unconscious heap. We straightened him out and left him to recover. The evening meal was served and consumed, though not by Harry who, stretched on his back, remained dead to the world. When it began to get dark we thought we had better try to rouse him. We shook him with some vigour but he only grunted. Water thrown on his face also failed to revive him so we carried him into the hut and laid him on his bedspace. He muttered again but nothing he said was understandable.

Shortly after bringing Harry inside, it was announced by a messenger from the orderly room that our party was to be ready to leave for Bangkok at midnight. This surprised us because no previous party had been moved during the hours of darkness. The authorities were obviously doing their best to recover the time lost through the visit of the Countess, so we had no complaint, but Harry was a problem. Throughout the evening we constantly tried to rouse him and after an hour or two he successfully answered the question

"How are you?"

"Not too bad, thanks," was his reply.

This encouraged us, but we were completely unable to keep him awake. He was still asleep when midnight came and the lorries arrived. We hauled Harry to a sitting position, shook him and again asked him how he was. He again replied

"Not too bad, thanks."

But he did not reply to our further question which was

"Can you make it to the lorry?"

It was thus clear that we were going to have to carry him. We accordingly slid him forward in the sitting position until his legs dangled over the edge of the sleeping platform. We then positioned ourselves on either side of him, placed his arms on our shoulders and hauled him upright. His legs were very weak and functioned only intermittently. This caused his toes to drag on the ground for most of the way and made our job extremely difficult, but we got him to the lorry and, while Mac went back for the kit, I propped Harry in a sitting position with his back to the cab. When all the lorries were loaded (there were about a dozen of them) engines were started and we were on our way home, or at least to Bangkok, which was a firm step in the right direction.

It was now raining and the lorries provided no cover, but our high spirits were unquenchable and we sang bawdy songs all the way to Bangkok. "The Ball of Kirriemuir", being a favourite, was repeated endlessly. In pauses between the songs. either Mac or I would put the vital question to Harry

"How are you now, Harry boy"

"Not too bad, thanks," Harry would reply. but with increasing firmness as the journey progressed.

It was dawn when we eventually drove up to the entrance of Bangkok airport and were halted and inspected by a troop of Gurkhas. By this time Harry was fully conscious, though not yet well enough to join the singing,. which continued until we got down from the lorries on reaching the airport buildings. We breakfasted and were then led out onto the tarmac where a line of Dakota aircraft were waiting to fly us to Rangoon.

Postscript

Of the 20 officers and 480 men originally comprising the British Battalion, 2 officers and 150 men died in captivity. The overall death rate was thus 30.4%, with a considerable disparity in favour of the officers. Corresponding figures for the whole of the Burma Railway are difficult to obtain but it would appear that the total number of prisoners employed was in the region of 62,000 of whom about 18,000 (or 29%) died. The experience of the British Battalion thus appears to have been typical, though there were no doubt variations from one group of prisoners to another.

The condition of prisoners who survived and returned home varied considerably. After a spell of good food and some basic medical attention, many appeared not to have suffered any serious damage but there were others who came home permanently disabled, either physically or mentally or both. Pensions were granted in some cases, but not if there was the slightest suspicion that the disability might have been caused other than by war service.

When I came home and was medically examined by the RAF it was discovered that I was carrying the nematode worm Strongyloides Stercoralis. Others were similarly affected and we were all treated with gentian violet, administered by mouth, but the fact that gentian violet was a useless remedy was not disclosed to us. We were consequently discharged believing that we were free of the worm when the authorities knew full well that the condition was incurable. This shabby act of concealment, which enabled the government to avoid granting pensions to those affected, did not emerge until 1980 when the department of Health and Social Security brought to the attention of General Practitioners the fact that a genuine cure had now been discovered.

In their statement, the DHSS urged the doctors to encourage all their patients who had been prisoners in the Far East, to undergo tests to determine whether or not the worm was present. It also warned that a Strongyloides sufferer, if given cortico steroids for some other ailment, might well develop hyperinfection which could prove fatal.

At about the same time as the DHSS made their statement, I also discovered that a principle symptom of the worm was a recurring skin rash, similar to nettle rash. I had been intermittently plagued by such a rash ever since the war and it left me in little doubt that the worm was still with me. I therefore lost no time in applying to the DHSS for the recommended examination and was duly admitted to the military hospital at Woolwich where I spent about a week, undergoing various tests. In the last of these, I was required to swallow a bullet shaped metal object attached to a length of string. This accomplished, not without some difficulty, the object then slid of its own accord gradually down to stomach level, where it was allowed to remain for some two or three hours, the end of the string meanwhile dangling from my mouth. The bullet was then hauled up and taken away for pathological examination. The result was positive and I was prescribed a course of Mintezol which is a proprietary form of Thiabendazole.

As a result of what was discovered at Woolwich, I was categorised by the DHSS as 6 to 14% disabled and given as "final settlement" a lump sum of £1409. Whether or not it was wise to accept a final settlement, only time will tell. The rash has certainly disappeared but the nature of the admitted 6 to 14% damage remains a mystery. This occasionally disturbs me but I am above all grateful that during the thirty-five years I carried the worm, I suffered no illness requiring cortisone treatment How many Strongyloides sufferers were prescribed this drug, and died as a result, will never be known.

But enough of Strongyloides, How do we who were prisoners of Japan regard that nation today? Despite the fact that it is now half a century since the war ended, most of us still strongly dislike and distrust the Japanese. We dislike them because they ill-treated us and were responsible for the wretched deaths of so many of our comrades, and we distrust them because we remember events such as Pearl Harbour and the hypocrisy of the "Greater South-East Asia Co-Prosperity Sphere". We see Japan as outwardly honourable and inwardly devious.

I recently watched a television programme in which it was put to a Japanese diplomat that there were still fears in the world that his country would one day again be tempted into military expansionism. His reply was that, just as Britain had renounced her Imperialist past, so had Japan. This, on the face of it, seems a fair statement, but it ignores the fact that, unlike Britain, Japan has the wealth to enable her to pursue an expansionist policy if she so chooses. It also ignores the fact that within convenient striking distance of Japan there are numerous far weaker nations, including Korea and Taiwan, both of which are former colonies of Japan.

Japan's wealth rests on huge trade surpluses with the rest of the world. These surpluses have constantly increased for many years and there is no sign whatever that this pattern will not continue. Japan is thus fast becoming, if she is not already, the richest (and therefore the most powerful) nation in the world.

Wealth alone, it may be argued, does not necessarily cause a nation to turn to militarism. This is true, but there are in fact very few instances in history of powerful nations not becoming belligerent, especially those with a militarist tradition (witness Germany in 1870, 1914 and 1939). But perhaps this is too pessimistic a view. Perhaps. in reality, history has nothing to teach us. There is, after all, the 1945 Peace Treaty with Japan which limits that country's arms expenditure to 1% of the gross domestic product. This surely is a firm enough restriction to keep Japan within bounds. It might be, if the United States had the will to enforce it, but she has not. She regularly allows the Japanese to exceed the 1% limit. and indeed encourages them to do so. The reason for this (apparently) is that, in American eyes, all capitalist nations are friendly and all socialist countries are enemies. This naive doctrine prevents America from understanding that there may well be capitalist enemies in Tokyo, not to mention Hiroshima and Nagasaki.

We in the West should also be concerned at Japan's recent decision to begin investing substantially in Space Research. The blunt fact is that mastery of space spells mastery of the world. The USA and the USSR were the chief competitors in the Space Race but Japan, with her superior technological ability (and endless wealth) is capable ultimately of outclassing both of these nations in this vital area of military science.

These views will not be shared by those who are too young to remember (or to have experienced) the depredations of Japan during the 1930's and 40's, but I strongly urge such people to take the trouble to study the history of this nation during those years.

SHEEPY PARVA   STANLEY SADDINGTON
LEICS. CV9 3RE